Traditional

Japanese

Design

FIVE

TASTES

Traditional

Japanese

Design

FIVE

TASTES

BY MICHAEL DUNN

JAPAN SOCIETY

HARRY N. ABRAMS, INC.

Traditional Japanese Design: Five Tastes is supported by Mitsubishi
International Corporation; Mitsui & Co. (USA), Inc.; Tiffany & Co.
Foundation; the Mary and James G. Wallach Foundation; the Lila
Wallace-Reader's Digest Endowment Fund; and the Friends of Japan
Society Gallery. Transportation is supported by Delta Airlines. ▲

This volume accompanies the exhibition *Traditional Japanese Design:
Five Tastes*, shown at Japan Society Gallery, New York, from September
26, 2001, through January 6, 2002. The exhibition is organized by
Japan Society, New York.

Traditional Japanese Design: Five Tastes
was produced for the Japan Society
by Perpetua Press, Los Angeles and Santa Barbara
Photo Editor: Annie Van Assche
Principal Photographers: John Bigelow Taylor and Dianne Dubler
Editors: Letitia O'Connor and Kathy Talley-Jones
Design: Dana Levy, Perpetua Press
Typeset in News Gothic
Manufactured by Toppan Printing Co., Tokyo

Library of Congress Card Number: 20010936698

Japan Society Gallery
333 East 47th Street
New York, NY 10017
www.japansociety.org
ISBN 0-913304-49-2 (Japan Society)

Distributed by Harry N. Abrams, Inc.
100 Fifth Avenue
New York, NY 10011
www.abramsbooks.com
ISBN 0-8109-6742-7 (Abrams)

Contents

Acknowledgments

Alexandra Munroe

T HE BOLD SIMPLICITY and graphic power of Japanese design have fascinated Western artists, architects, and designers since the wave of Japonisme first hit European shores in the late nineteenth century. *Traditional Japanese Design: Five Tastes* celebrates the forms, textures, and graphic images that have so inspired modern design worldwide and offers new ways of looking at the arts of Japan that merit sustained future research.

Where most Japanese craft and design shows have been organized by media or limited to a single expression, such as folk art, this is the first survey in America to approach traditional Japanese design from the cultural and aesthetic perspective of "taste." The five tastes that we explore evolved primarily from and correspond to the daily life and culture of Japan's dominant social classes of the Edo (1615–1868) and Meiji (1868–1912) periods—farmers, the ruling military elite, artisans, and merchants. Drawn from the canon of Japanese aesthetics and codified by influential twentieth-century cultural critics, these tastes offer contexts for appreciating Japan's design culture: Artless Simplicity *(Soboku)*, Zen Austerity *(Wabi)*, Gorgeous Splendor *(Karei)*, and Edo Chic *(Iki)*. An introductory section, Ancient Times *(Kodai no bi)*, focuses on archaeological materials that evoke the magic and mystery of native Japanese culture and suggest a link from the ancient world of ritual life to the mainstream of traditional Japanese culture. Our presentation also expands the conventional boundaries of Japanese object design (usually limited to work by "the unknown craftsman") to include objects of "high craft" like spectacular arms and armor and extraordinary textiles.

The exercise of Japanese taste, like that of any other culture, is an expression of personal, even eccentric, aesthetic ideas. The five tastes explored here are less categories by which to inventory style or form than contexts for understanding their visual appeal. Their boundaries are not defended and some objects may easily migrate from one group to another. Oribe ceramic ware, for example, appears as *wabi* in the form of an irregular, deep-black tea bowl; as *karei* in the form of a hot-water ewer richly decorated with maple leaves; and as *iki* in the form of five cups displaying an elegant geometric pattern. The ambiguity of this approach is further complicated by the appropriation of tastes among and across the different social classes. The cultural aesthetes who defined the *wabi* aesthetic in tea adapted the humble utensils of rural life, collected here as *soboku*, to use in their sophisticated tea rooms. And the wealthy merchants of the mid-to-late Edo period were quick to acquire the daimyo taste for sumptuous lacquer and textile decoration. The assignments suggested here are neither inevitable nor scientific. Rather, they offer an invitation to explore the craft arts of Japan from a different, if unfixed, perspective—a perspective that we hope will sharpen our appreciative eye.

Susan Sontag has written that taste, or sensibility, is distinct from an idea and therefore one of the hardest things to describe well. "Any sensibility which can be crammed into the mold of a system, or handled with the rough tools of proof, is no longer a sensibility at all. It has hardened into an idea...to snare a sensibility in words, especially one that is alive and powerful, one must be tentative and nimble." We hope our explorations of some complex sensibilities of Japanese culture will be tentative enough to inspire further looking and nimble enough to draw a wider circle still toward the riches of traditional Japanese culture.

Traditional Japanese Design: Five Tastes would not have been possible without the generosity of several important institutional and private lenders in the United States and Europe who are listed on page 10. We are grateful to all our lenders for their superb loans and the connoisseurship that have made this project possible.

Five Tastes has drawn on the dedicated talents and committed support of many individuals. We offer our greatest thanks to our exhibition curator, Michael Dunn, long-time resident of Japan and contributing author to *The Art of East Asia* (Könemann 1999). Michael's special familiarity with Japanese culture and his unerring eye have shaped this project in a most creative way. Organizing a project of this magnitude across an ocean and continent is always a challenge, and we are grateful for Michael's perfect charm and wise calm throughout our work together.

Several colleagues and friends have given generous counsel and guidance to this exhibition. We are especially grateful to Richard Danziger for helping us define the amorphous perimeters of Japanese taste with keen questions and insights. Others who helped Michael Dunn in his explorations are Dr. William Gater, Joseph La Penta, Jeffrey Montgomery, Donald Richie, Kazuko Shiomi, and Takeuchi Jun'ichirō. We are also grateful to Martin Lorber, whose familiarity with arms and armor helped our study in that area, and to Louise Alison Cort, Curator of Ceramics, Freer Gallery of Art and Arthur M. Sackler Gallery, who opened doors for us onto the ceramic world. We also thank scholars in Japan who offered valuable comments and answered queries relating to our textile research including Maruyama Nobuhiko, Assistant Professor, Kanazawa College of Art. For expertise in translation of texts that appear on certain garments, we thank John T. Carpenter, Lecturer, School of Oriental and African Studies, University of London, and Nobuko Ochner, Associate Professor of Japanese, and Eriko Iijima, Librarian, University of Hawaii. We were also fortunate to have two anonymous Japanese art experts dedicate much time and effort to all the catalogue texts. Their thoughtful insights and scholarship were an invaluable contribution to this publication.

Among our museum colleagues, several curators and conservators supported our research with generous expertise. At the Metropolitan Museum of Art, Sondra Castile, Conservator, Asian Art Conservation, and Nobuko Kajitani, Conservator in Charge, Textile Conservation, facilitated our collections research and advised masterfully on the installation of art in the Gallery; and Joyce Denney, Senior Research Assistant, Department of Asian Art, offered expertise at every stage of our textile research and writing. Others who deserve special thanks are Amy Poster, Curator and Chair, Department of Asian Art, and Frances Yuan, Assistant Curator, Department of Asian Art, the Brooklyn Museum of Art; Ann Morse, Curator of Japanese Art, the Museum of Fine Arts, Boston; Andrew Maskey, Associate Curator of Japanese Art, the Peabody Essex Museum; Felice Fischer, Luther W. Brady Curator of Japanese Arts, and Dilys Blum, Curator of Costume and Textiles, the Philadephia Museum of Art.

We are fortunate to have among our catalogue authors several eminent scholars of Japanese art and keen observers of Japanese culture. In addition to Mr. Dunn's texts, this catalogue features a preface by renowned weaver, designer, and collector, Jack Lenor Larsen, who writes of his personal passion for Japanese design and the life-long inspiration he has drawn from Japanese culture. We are fortunate to feature as well an introductory essay by Donald Richie, the internationally acclaimed author of numerous books on Japanese film, design, and culture. His perceptive survey of Japanese taste sheds light on the complexities of definition while focusing on those who created and lived for a life of aesthetic pleasures. Other contributors include Edward J. Kidder, Jr., professor emeritus of International Christian University, Tokyo, and a leading scholar of Japanese archaeology; Morihiro Ogawa, Senior Research Associate, the Metropolitan Museum of Art, and a foremost scholar of Japanese arms and armor; and textile specialist Annie Van Assche, Curator of Education, Japan Society Gallery. We are grateful to all these fine specialists for their enthusiastic embrace and persuasive articulation of the exhibition themes. We also thank Motoko Sakamoto for translating Mr. Ogawa's texts.

Our schedule posed special problems to our editor and designer, and it is with much admiration that we offer thanks to Letitia B. O'Connor and Dana Levy of Perpetua Press, Los Angeles and Santa Barbara. Mr. Levy—a renowned photographer and designer of books on Japanese subjects and co-curator of Japan Society's 1983 exhibition, *Kanban: Shop Signs of Japan*—has created an elegant design that should make *Five Tastes* a classic. At Japan Society Gallery, Annie Van Assche's tireless research has helped make *Five Tastes* a fine contribution to the expanding study of Japanese textiles. Finally, the talents of our principal photographer, John Bigelow Taylor, deserve high praise and much appreciation.

At Japan Society Gallery, Deputy Director Marilyn Simon ably oversaw the project's realization, and Assistant to the Director Hyunsoo Woo facilitated myriad jobs essential to our successful presentation. The assembly of the exhibition loans and their installation in our galleries has been administered by Nancy McGary and Eleni Cocordas, former and present Exhibitions Manager of the Gallery. Architects Tim Culbert and Celia Imrey have transformed the space of Japan Society Gallery and presented the objects of this show—and their special cultural contexts—to extraordinary effect. In Jeff Nemeth, who oversees the fabrication of our installations, we have a manager of countless skills. We also thank our publicist, Ruth Kaplan, who has ably supported our vision to bring Japan Society Gallery's activities to the attention of a broad and vital public.

Since its founding in 1971, Japan Society Gallery has been a preeminent venue for exhibitions of Japanese design and crafts. These include some of the Gallery's most popular shows ever, such as

Tsutsumu: The Art of Japanese Wrapping (1979); *Kanban: Shop Signs of Japan* (1983); *Kawari Kabuto: Spectacular Helmets of Japan, 16th–19th Century* (1985); and *Japanese Folk Art: A Triumph of Simplicity* (1992). *Traditional Japanese Design: Five Tastes* builds on this history while pushing open the doors of inquiry a little wider still. This project could not have been realized but for the leadership of Japan Society's president, William Clark, Jr., whose encouragement sustains our explorations. I am also grateful to John Wheeler, Carl Schellhorn, Elizabeth Costa, Diana Foster, and Heather Junker of the Japan Society for their support of, and key role in, the development and realization of this project. Finally, I offer gratitude to the Gallery's Art Advisory Committee, chaired by Samuel Sachs II, for its support and counsel on all aspects of the Gallery's programming.

Japan Society is grateful for the support of corporate, foundation, and individual funding that made this exhibition and publication possible. We acknowledge Mitsubishi International Corporation; Mitsui & Co. (USA), Inc.; Tiffany & Co.; the Mary and James G. Wallach Foundation; and at Japan Society, the Lila Wallace-Reader's Digest Endowment Fund. We thank Delta Airlines for supporting our transportation. We are especially grateful to the Friends of Japan Society Gallery for their leadership and vision in all aspects of the Gallery's programming.

ALEXANDRA MUNROE
Director, Japan Society Gallery

Lenders to the Exhibition

Asia Society

Brooklyn Museum of Art

Lloyd and Margit Cotsen Collection

Peggy and Richard M. Danziger Collection

Kay and Tom Edson Collection

Victor and Takako Hauge Collection

The Florence and Herbert Irving Collection

Jack Lenor Larsen Collection

The Metropolitan Museum of Art

Jeffrey Montgomery Collection

Museum of Fine Arts, Boston

Peabody Essex Museum

Philadelphia Museum of Art

Steven and Jacqueline Strelitz Collection

John C. Weber Collection

Private Collections

The Inspiration of Japanese Design

Jack Lenor Larsen

|F, TO MY MIND, there remain some vague outer limits defining good design and worthy craft, these have over the years widened considerably—in all arts, including performing ones. But isn't this one of the deep pleasures of growing up and older: to perceive value in ever widening ranges of art?

For decades now I have laughed at my own sophomoric canon of aesthetic purity when only Mondrian and Bach were placed on the highest altar. Such austerity demanded moral judgments, as well. With young comrades I frowned on polished woods and cut stones, luxury furs, and most trappings of the anciennes regimes. Then, without abandoning satisfaction with such pure forms as eggs and daisies, cubes and candles, I found this weaver's hands and eyes becoming sensitive to distinctions among silks and straws, wiry linens and toothy homespuns. With this developed an appreciation of quality—of finesse and nuance. Perhaps experiencing exotic foods first nourished my notion of a connoisseurship beyond indulgence. After shedding wardrobes to focus on spiritual values, I learned from a teacher that a few appropriate wearables may express, not vanity, but a gift to the viewers; in other words, an art form.

To me, then, art came off of its pedestal to appear as a volatile essence potentially in all life's forms, as pertinent to a gesture or the turning of a phrase as a full evening's performance. As I learned that art, therefore design and craft, have much to do with grace and generosity, I saw how quickly beauty retreats from pretense, imitation, and the grandiose.

Of course, modesty, economy, and simplicity were all core virtues of Modernism with its emphasis on expressing structure, materials, and function. Modern, in postwar Puget Sound where I came of age, was personally scaled and residential, with the sloping rooflines of houses reflecting hillsides as discreetly as their Japanese precedents. Inside, small paintings of Mark Tobey or Morris Graves were as unobtrusive as hanging scrolls. For me, Modernism and Japonism came together as influences guiding the metamorphosis of my aspirations, from being an architect to becoming a weaver *for* architecture.

In God's Country, as we thought of it then, that misty frontier closer to Japan than Europe, middle-class conformity was as pervasive as our rain clouds. As a bulwark against this norm, the artists, architects, designers, craftmakers, and lumber barons formed a tightly knit, supportive alliance. As I was to see later in Japan, there was no hierarchy among creators, and craftmakers were held in high regard.

I recognized two pervasive influences as a student. One remained the Northwest Coast Indian art I had known since I spent rainy days of childhood inside a museum. The carved cedar and especially the twined basketry became even more instructive as I began to weave and study anthropology. The other presence, East Asia and particularly Japan, was in the air. Our school libraries were rich in old art books printed there. I also came to know some of the Japanese we students helped in their return from war camps or at the Japan Town eateries favored by our painters. Comfortable with their gentle modesty, I was impressed by the easy generosity of those with so little.

My introduction to Japanese taste was deepened as I became friends with the painter Mark Tobey. "I've never met a weaver before but I know two potters!" (Mark had spent two years in Japan with Bernard Leach and Shoji Hamada.) He taught me how to hold a tea bowl with ten fingers—for tea, clear soup, even coffee—and how to perceive objects sometimes costly but often found. "Don't look until I have it against a gray wall!" This so I would read the content, not just its contrasting outline. "No, don't blow off the dust!" So, mother's tenets were replaced by Mark's invitation to inner spaces where the obvious did not much matter. "Close your eyes and <u>feel</u> it! Sense it. Understand its making and quality until you know in your bones the essence! And when you really know the nature of this steel, this camphor wood, that jade, and the clay pot in your hand, you may, one day, understand even yourself and your place among others and under heaven."

Since my early days with Mark Tobey, I have traveled often and too quickly to Japan and the East. I have seen great beauty in temples and gardens, ceramics, lacquer, garments, and tools; I have met serious masters. Old and new Japan remains my favorite country, a place of inspiration.

Although the Japanese aesthetic is sometimes described as Minimalist I don't see it that way. If traditional rooms appear to be unfurnished, they are rich in composition, in relationship to each other, and to a controlled view. This visual restraint puts the focus on the caring craftsmanship with which each medium is worked. In these "empty" spaces one observes with heightened awareness the single flower in a vase, some poetic calligraphy on a scroll, others in the room with you—all within a sustaining serenity.

Craftmakers working within Japan's ancient traditions respond to the generations of passed-on knowledge. This collective memory includes a deep respect for material and process, and respect too for the intended user. Objects of Japanese design and craft serve with grace, simplicity, and discipline a single form or purpose. Nothing on a Japanese sword, however ornamental, competes with the curve, its single dominant expression. A ceramic container, however masterful, is subordinate to the flowers—the art—it is designed to support.

Creations of Japanese craft remain high among those art forms I respond to on the deepest level, and are the most compelling as instructors. That they possess at least implied function makes them the more available, like old friends. "Hey, I know you. We once worked together!"

Distillation is an aspect of Japanese art that appeals deeply to me. Where a European object may be decorated all over, a Japanese piece will have one mark (such as the fire marking on a pot or a graphic symbol)—and it will be the right one. I so admire this reticence, this distaste for any effulgence, that allows a single aspect—surface, symbol, or color—to dominate.

Restraint describes the essence of Japanese chic too. It requires a trained response, generations of aristocratic understatement, to understand the beauty of an undergarment that is ten times more valuable that an outer robe, or mark the subtle differences of one pattern from another. It is a perfection of nuance, a ripeness, a superb unawareness. Like a great actress who can throw away her lines, Japanese style is sure and casual.

Between Good Sense and Good Taste

Donald Richie

Entre le bon sens and le bon goût il y a la différence de la cause et son effet.
Between good sense and good taste there is the same difference as between cause and effect.

JEAN DE LA BRUYERE (1645–1696)

PRECISELY—although it was said by a Frenchman and our subject is Japanese. Still, in matters aesthetic the world over, taste is the observation of deserved worth and that should define the matter, except that we are not all agreed as to what good sense consists of.

Some cultures say one thing, some say another. The Japanese traditionally say that we have been given a standard to use. It is there, handy, daily: this is nature itself, things as they are. Nature makes good sense, the only sense, really, and it should be our model. We are to regard it, to learn from it.

This observation makes such sense that one would have expected it to apply to everyone everywhere, but this is not so. In *Literary and Art Theories of Japan*, the eminent Japanese aesthetician, Makoto Ueda, noted: "In premodern Japanese aesthetics the distance between art and nature was considerably shorter than in its Western counterparts."[1]

Elsewhere—Europe, even sometimes in China—nature was there as guide, but its role was restricted to mimesis, realistic reproduction. In Japan this was not enough. It was as though an agreement existed here that the nature of nature could not be presented through literal description. It could only be suggested and the more subtle the suggestion (think of haiku), the more tasteful the work of art.

Here Japanese arts and crafts (a distinction the premodern Japanese did not themselves observe) imitated the means of nature rather than its results. One of the means was simplicity. There is nothing ornate about nature: every branch, twig, leaf counts structurally. Showing structure, emphasizing texture—even boldly displaying an almost ostentatious lack of artifice—this was what the Japanese learned to do.

This simplicity was found beautiful, and that is a prerequisite for taste. Although a Japanese word for aesthetics was coined only late in the nineteenth century, beauty is taken seriously indeed—so seriously that one might say a word was not needed for its study until the modern world had already begun its process of uglification.

There is beauty to be found in texture and grain, in naked structure, also in the precise stroke of the inked brush, the perfect judo throw, the rightness of placing a single flower. This beauty is both the expression and the result of an awareness that comes from an open regard of nature and an accompanying discipline, which is one of the reasons that the arts are rarely casual in Japan.

But such a subjective term as beauty (even under a rubric as generous as good sense equals good taste) needs to be codified. Though Japan is much more interested in (and better at) synthesis than analysis, some means of cataloguing are necessary if one is to understand (and explain) the aesthetic impulse. It is thus that Japanese good taste was early divided into a number of tastes, five of which have been chosen for consideration here. All share qualities in common, despite their differences.

Consider that courtly taste for grace and refinement which we call elegance. Natural to its roots, elegance flowers—and these graceful blooms have been given names: *yugen, iki, furyū*.

❖ ❖ ❖

Let us examine this last, *furyū*. Historically this quality is associated with Ashikaga Yoshimasa, who ruled from 1449 to 1473 and by his actions helped define it. Just what this quality is, however, is open to some interpretation. The dictionary offers "elegant, tasteful, refined, graceful, artistic, aesthetic," but English has no precise equivalent. Yoshimasa's example gives a better idea of the meaning of the term.

He had led a full and active political life and was sick of it. The fifteenth century in Japan was just one civil war after another. So, if the shogun could not make peace in the political realm, he sought it in the spiritual. He cultivated the unostentatious, the subdued, the meditative—more important elements of *furyū* than elegance and refinement. Yoshimasa had learned that anything perfect arouses the acquisitive instinct. Therefore all of his buildings, gardens, even his vases and plates, were made (with a wonderful natural grace, it is true) of the plainest materials, the materials of nature itself.

In Western terms we may substitute the basic black Chanel suit, full of *furyū* —or would be if it were made of less expensive fabric; native African pottery, refined over generations but made of the same common earth, has the quality; so does the music of Erik Satie, composed as it is of common harmonies cunningly juxtaposed, the most unadored melody sculpted with style.

Furyū has something else in addition: when Japanese objects exhibiting this quality are brought together, they create a special kind of atmosphere, the essence of which is a sort of assured serenity. Listening to Satie while wearing a Chanel suit and looking at a Bantu pot would not have the same effect, because it is a cultural mishmash. To exist beautifully in an environment composed of nothing but the most elegant simplicity is an aesthetic ideal that is defined for Japanese culture by *furyū*; in other cultures, a similar impulse manifests itself differently.

A resulting craze for the natural, an ostentatious rush for the unostentatious, which developed following Yoshimasa's aristocratic example, might be partially explained by the congruence between the concept of *furyū* and both the basic Buddhist doctrine that this man-made world is delusion and the equally strong Japanese belief that the only way to live in this world is to subject oneself to its natural immutable laws.

This thought is not unknown in the West. For example, the seventeenth-century English poet Edmund Waller compares his beloved to a rose and then, in fine Japanese fashion, tells the flower to be his messenger, to go and die before her eyes "that she the common fate of all things rare may read in thee." For, "how small a part of time they share, that are so wondrous sweet and fair."

A Japanese would have instantly understood, that the poem by no means issues an invitation to gather ye rosebuds while ye may. Rather, it acknowleges the transcience of all things, but it also attempts to find beauty and consolation in this acknowledgment. Many people everywhere spend their whole lives trying to escape the knowledge that one day they and all of theirs will be no more. Only a few poets look at the fact, and only the Japanese, I believe, celebrated it. This celebration takes many forms, but the most common would be to look into a mirror, see one more gray hair, discern one more wrinkle, and then reassure oneself: "Good, all is well with the world; things are proceeding as they must."

This attitude (the opposite of going to the beauty parlor) also gives pleasure, the pleasure of discovering a corroboration of this great and natural law of change in one's own face. Recognition of natural process in the outside world can be appreciated as a disassociated and satisfied melancholy. Cherry blossoms are thus preferred not when they are at their fullest but afterwards, when the air is thick with their falling petals, and so with the unavoidable reminder that they too have had their day and must rightly perish.

Immortality, in that it is considered at all, is to be found through nature's way. The form is kept though the contents evaporate. Permanance through materials (granite, marble, the pyramids) is seldom attempted in native Japanese aesthetics, where the claims of immortality were honored in another way. Here the paradigm would be the shrine of Ise, made of common wood, razed every twenty years, and at the same time identically rebuilt in a neighboring plot. Permanence is celebrated only in frankly expiring examples.

This reveals a prime quality of the Japanese notion of beauty: not only should the aesthetic be natural, it should also be impermanent. This appreciation of the evanescent could also, as Makoto Ueda reminds us, "be considered a variation of elegance, for exquisite beauty is fragile and apt easily to perish." This concept is elaborated as *aware* and *mono no aware*, a construct that despite various valiant attempts cannot be translated into English. Ueda's paraphrase is long, but gives some idea of a concept is so important to traditional Japanese aesthetics that Murasaki Shikibu uses the term more than a thousand times in the *Tale of Genji*: "a deep, empathetic appreciation of the ephermal beauty manifest in nature and human life, and therefore usually tinged with a hint of sadness [though] under certain circumstances it can be accompanied by admiration, awe, or even joy."[2]

Such categorization of aesthetics cannot be too successfully accomplished in the West—though Plato, Hegel, Kant, and many others attempted to. Those aestheticians were forced to use such imprecise terms as "soul" and "spirit" and "the ineffable." In Japanese, however, a language sometimes seemingly more vague than most, there is apparently no such problem. Aesthetic categories thrive; and categories within categories.

One of these subcategories is mentioned here, both because it is sometimes overlooked and because it gives some insight into the Japanese aesthetic sense at work. Within the tastes there operates another system of categorization, which describes the "mood" of whatever it is: flower arrangement, the manner of holding a tea bowl, the quality of writing itself, kimono pattern, tatami binding, a way of walking or even standing, other forms of creation and comport. It is an agreed-upon tripartite system of categorization (*shin-gyo-so*) used to convey emotional states and one that early aestheticians hoped would cover all such moods and their reflections.

The first term *shin*, covers things formal, slow, symmetrical, imposing. The third, *so*, is applied to things informal, fast, asymmetrical, relaxed. *Gyo* describes everything that falls between the extremes of the other two. For instance, the Washington Monument is *shin*: symmetrical, formal, correct, official, imposing, and at the same time almost elaborately beautiful. We have no official public monuments in this style that could be characterized as *so* (all of them being *shin* by definition of being monuments), but a Frank Lloyd Wright house might serve to define this model. It is asymmetrical, informal and relaxed in this style, and at the same time both simple and beautiful.

This tripartite system of categorization is used in Japan to describe the differing moods of calligraphy and ink paintings, the way one might in the West contrast formal, informal, and hastily cursive handwriting. Another application of this structure was observed by flower-master Teshighara Sōfu, who said that *shin* describes a traditional *tokonoma* alcove, floored with tatami mats, its main post lacquered, and all of its proportions exact and formal, but for a *tokonoma* to be *gyo*, it would be floored with wood, its grain still showing, and its post perhaps a natural tree trunk. He said he had never heard of a *tokonoma* in the *so* manner, as they are simply not made that way, but surely the rudimentary *tokonoma* of some rustic tea-ceremony hut somewhere might theoretically approach *so* in its informality.

There are also a number of combinations, which are applied to varying intermediary degrees of the three moods. There is the *so* of *shin*, the *so* of *gyo*, and the *so* of *so*, for example. (Hemingway would probably be the *so* of *gyo*, while Faulkner would perhaps be the *so* of *shin*.) There are nine such combinations in all—like the nine postures of the Amida Buddha—and the collective Japanese word for this process is *santai kyushi* (three bodies, nine forms.)

All of this aesthetic terminology might seem pettifogging to the Westerner, but like constructions exist in many cultures and serve the same purpose—as some secret codes. Formulations like the *shin-gyo-so* triptych serve as shorthand in the discussion of a complicated art.

The Japanese of the fifteenth century—like those of twenty-first and all centuries in between—delighted in such rules. When people gathered and talked about such things, the atmosphere perhaps resembled some chic New York or Paris opening with recently acquired apparel being showed off and much connoisseur talk about the merits of this or that—whether the pot or the bowl or the ikebana showed the *shin* of *shin* or merely the *gyo* of *shin*. Still, the emotion called for, the real reason for the party, is familiar: it is the pursuit of beauty.

❖   ❖   ❖

On such an occasion a standard of taste is agreed upon. Good taste is thus a shared discovery, which fast shades into a conviction. It may have its origin in the unpeopled world of nature itself, but it soon enters good society.

In Japan, particularly from the seventeenth century on, Yoshimasa's private if courtly formulations became those of moneyed folk at large. The quality of *iki*, which is one of the Five Tastes that structure this exhibition and has been defined for this audience as Edo Chic, is based upon this social agreement. As Ueda has pointed out, *iki* not only expresses an aesthetic, it also represents a moral ideal. "Aesthetically… pointed toward an urbane, chic, bourgeois type of beauty with undertones of sensuality. Morally…envisioned the tasteful life of a person who was wealthy but not attached to money, who enjoyed sensual pleasure but was never carried away by carnal desires."[3]

All of this has now had its day. *Iki* turns into cool, nature is put on the back burner, and method becomes media. Hence, then, the value of looking back along the long corridors of history and glimpsing a world where beauty was sought, where its qualities could be classified, and where a word for aesthetics was not necessary. Our Five Tastes, like Miyamoto Musashi's five rings, indicate a method and still something of a hope. Though it does not seem likely, Jean de la Bruyere's dictum yet holds: to enjoy good taste we only have to decide, for ourselves, what good sense is.

1. Makoto Ueda, *Literary and Art Theories of Japan* (Ann Arbor: Center for Japanese Studies, University of Michigan, 1991).

2. Ibid

3. Ibid

A Discussion of Japanese Taste

Michael Dunn

ARLY IN LIFE, the primary meaning of the word "taste" is learned together with the gradual awareness of the five senses, but the other, more extended meaning—"the faculty of discerning and enjoying beauty and other excellence, especially in art and literature, or appropriateness of conduct"[1]—is understood with maturity and experience. The first meaning is sensual and intensely personal and can vividly evoke memories. The second is more intellectual than impressionistic in nature and can therefore be somewhat distanced from the self and its feelings. In his book, *Reflections on Japanese Taste: The Structure of Iki* (one of the early attempts to analyze Japanese taste), the modern philosopher Kuki Shūzō writes, "These senses of taste, touch, and smell form the essential meaning of experience. The so-called higher senses develop as senses at a distance; they separate things from the self, and objectively oppose things to the self."[2] It follows that the recognition of good taste is one thing, but the expression of good taste is another matter altogether.

"Good taste" and "bad taste" are familiar enough terms, but their meanings are perceived variously according to nationality or ethnicity, education or cultural milieu. Even within similar groups, a uniform understanding of the meaning of these terms is as elusive as it is, perhaps, undesirable. In undertaking this exhibition and book, *Traditional Japanese Design: Five Tastes,* I have assumed the stance that ultimately taste is born of, yet can transcend, background; that an appreciation of certain cultural and intellectual ideas can cross time.

In traditional Japanese culture, taste connotes æsthetics—the appreciation and philosophy of beauty and art—an area long defined by the assiduous pursuit of excellence. The Japanese language is rich in words used to indicate many subtle nuances of taste. For example, the word *suki* has a more-or-less similar meaning to the English word "taste," but with a connotation of curiosity—or even eccentricity—in matters of artistic discernment. *Suki* is a word often associated with *chanoyu,* the tea ceremony and its practice: *sukidogu* are tastefully selected objects (particularly tea utensils); *sukiya* architecture is that refined but rustic style seen in tea rooms and the residences of tea connoisseurs; and *sukisha* connotes a person with recognized good taste. The word *konomi* has a similar meaning but is more universal, not restricted to the world of tea and its æsthetes, and it emphasizes the role of choice and selection in demonstrating taste—and the pleasure that comes with finding particularly satisfying objects. *Gashu,* another word used to mean tasteful, has a nuance of refinement and sophisticated elegance.

The Japanese sense of beauty is essentially an æsthetic of feelings, as the etymology of its vocabulary reveals. One of the Japanese words meaning "beautiful," *utsukushii,* evolved from original meaning of "being loved" during the Muromachi period (1336–1568) to assume the idea of "beauty" that it connotes today. According to art historian Takashina Shūji, the Japanese sense of beauty is based more in emotion than in intellect. Takashina also states that the Japanese aesthetic shuns what is large, powerful, or abundant, and shows no inclination to reduce beauty to such rationalist rules as symmetry, proportion, or geometry, refusing such formulas as the golden section that has defined Western standards of beauty since ancient Greece. "Beauty has not been perceived as an intrinsic attribute of a given object, but as something that exists in the mind that perceives it."[3] Another word for beauty is *kirei,* which also evolved during the Muromachi period, adding that sense to its original meaning of "clean." Takashina cites the linguist Ōno Susumu in concluding that, "the Japanese have in their perception of beauty tended to sympathize with things that are clear, clean, pure, or small, rather than with things that represent goodness or abundance."[4]

How such a refined sense of beauty has survived in the midst of the industrial blight that afflicts much of Japan is further evidence that values can transcend time. But if design requires the human touch to be imbued with the quality of taste, the sad prospect arises that, as almost everything today is mass-produced by machines, æsthetic taste may soon follow the fate of sensory taste and be abandoned by the wayside of evolution. Similar developments have been documented in other areas of the world, and socioeconomic reasons abound to explain them. Perhaps because the Japanese possess the extraordinary ability to edit out, in the mind's eye, all that is not necessary, these parallel worlds can coexist. Thus a simple arrangement of wild flowers can be fully appreciated, its beauty savored, without the impression being sullied by the neighboring air-conditioning unit. An enviable gift....

❖   ❖   ❖

This exhibition identifies five areas of taste to explore by looking at traditional Japanese crafts and design of the preindustrial period. These groupings vary according to the age or milieu in which they flourished, but their borders are amorphous and overlap in many ways. The objects, made for daily use by townspeople, the aristocracy, cultural aesthetes, as well as farmers and fishermen, are drawn primarily from the Edo (1615–1868) and Meiji (1868–1912) periods, with an introductory section presenting tools and vessels from Japan's prehistoric Jōmon, Yayoi, and Kofun eras. Ancient Times (*Kodai no bi*) features select archaeological objects—such as stone tools, funerary jewelry, and bold ceramics with natural-ash glazes—whose forms illustrate the origins of Japan's native genius for design. This taste, which provided modern artists like Okamoto Tarō with an inspiration similar to that the "primitivism" of African art once provided to Picasso and Matisse, evokes a nativist fascination with the cultures of Japan's archaic past. Artless Simplicity (*Soboku*) connotes a taste that is rustic, unadorned, and sober. This section includes objects that were made for a rural culture where simple, local materials were used with economy and function in mind. Its origins date to medieval times, but expanded to a new audience in the early twentieth century, when a taste for everyday objects made by unknown craftsmen was championed by Yanagi Sōetsu, who founded Japan's folk art movement in the 1920s

Among the most refined concepts in Japanese culture, *wabi* is linked to the aesthetics of Zen and used primarily in connection with tea masters—aesthetes and connoisseurs of the spiritual beauty found in objects that are worn, natural, and of humble origin. The articulation of Zen Austerity *(Wabi)* is attributed to the late sixteenth-century tea master, Sen no Rikyū, whose stringent, radical aesthetics profoundly shaped Japanese architecture, garden design, and many of the craft arts. It was promoted in the twentieth century by the aesthete Okakura Kakuzō, author of *The Book of Tea*, and the Zen philosophers D. T. Suzuki and Hisamatsu Shin'ichi—all of whose writings influenced modern international art and design.

The term Gorgeous Splendor *(Karei)* invokes the magnificent culture associated with the nobility and ruling warrior elite, but wealthy merchants of the mid-to-late Edo period also took on aspects of *karei* taste. In contrast to the simplicity and minimalism of the objects that express *soboku* or *wabi*, the pieces in this section demonstrate the refined skills of traditional Japanese craftsmanship and display a bold, decorative surface design. Rich decorative patterns, designed to enthrall the viewer with virtuoso craftsmanship and sumptuous ornamentation, are found on rare *kosode* robes and lacquer and ceramic wares representative of this taste.

Finally, the essentially urban concept of *iki* conjures the smart style of Edo-period townspeople and their "floating world," which found expression in the kabuki theater and pleasure quarters. Edo Chic developed with the appearance of the wealthy merchant class and is personified by the dandy and courtesan who frequent popular literature and ukiyo-e woodblock prints of the eighteenth and ninteenth centuries. Restricted by sumptuary laws that prohibited conspicuous consumption, the Edo townspeople created objects ingeniously designed to conceal rather than reveal extravagance. A vanguard taste in Japanese urban culture, *iki* is most often expressed in fashion style, through the understated elegance of small, geometric patterns on textiles whose graphic simplicity belies their high craftsmanship. Other examples are exotic accessories or ones that hint at their outrageous cost, like a smoking set by the lacquer artist Zeshin that includes a tobacco pouch fashioned from an imported Southeast Asian textile (Plate 73).

In Japanese as in English, tastes can be expressed as metaphors for the original sensory experience of sensing flavors. We are used to describing music as hot or cool, individuals as salty or sweet, attitudes and experiences as bitter or sour. Similar usage is seen in Japanese: the traditional five tastes (*go-mi*—spicy-hot, vinegary-sour, bitter-astringent, sweet, and salty—can be extended to the five selected aesthetic tastes. One might propose, for example, that the antiquity and religious purity of *kodai* evokes a certain saltiness, while *wabi* is definitely bitter-astringent (*shibui*). *Iki* also shows *shibui* qualities together with sweetness and, at times, a hot spiciness in its complex ethos, while *karei* taste can be seen as sweet in a domestic setting, salty and bitter on the battlefield. With its rustic origins, *soboku* suggests bitter and salty flavors over any others.

Of course, there are other tastes than these five. The taste for the grotesque can also manifest itself in the high arts, as seen in the genre of Buddhist hell depictions (*jigoku-ha*) of the Kamakura period (1185–1392) or in much of the graphic work of the artist Hokusai (1760–1849). A preference for loud, showy colors and patterns (*hade*) is a well-known element of Japanese culture, especially among those involved in the kabuki theater. However central these and other terms are to an understanding of the full spectrum of Japanese aesthetic tastes, they are more relevant to areas other than design.

Japanese aesthetic sensibilities are, like any other, difficult to contain in a single definition. In his essay on *wabi, sabi,* and *suki,* cultural critic Itoh Teiji has written, "The problem is that our attempts to bring these concepts out into the open do little to demystify them. Still, it would be a mistake to conclude that therefore most Japanese do not really understand the meaning of these terms. The dilemma we face is that our grasp is intuitive and perceptual, rather than rational and logical."[5]

A similar sentiment is echoed by Susan Sontag in her influential text, "Notes on Camp," where she uses the word "taste" as a synonym for sensibility and asserts that "taste has no system and no proofs." In addressing the sheer difficulty of writing about taste, she proposes that: "Any sensibility which can be crammed into the mold of a system, or handled with the rough tools of a proof, is no longer a sensibility at all. It has hardened into an idea…To snare a sensibility in words, especially one that is alive and powerful, one must be tentative and nimble."[6] Very true—and is it not significant that for the past six hundred years or so, the flavor that most permeates Japanese culture is that of Zen spirituality, which by its very practice, abandons the rational and seeks understanding through intuition?

1. *The Concise Oxford Dictionary* defines taste thus; *Websters* emphasizes "critical judgment, discernment, or appreciation."
2. Kuki Shūzō, *Reflections on Japanese Taste: The Structure of Iki.* Translated by John Clark; edited by John Clark and Sakuko Matsui (Sydney: Power Publications, 1997), p. 112.
3. Takashina Shūji, "The Japanese Sense of Beauty" in *Autumn Grasses and Water Motifs in Japanese Art.* (New York: Japan Society; Tokyo: Suntory Museum of Art, 1983) pp. 10 -11.
4. *ibid.* p.10
5. Teiji Itoh, *Wabi, Sabi, Suki: The Essence of Japanese Culture.* Hiroshima: Mazda Motor Corporation. 1993.
6. Susan Sontag, "Notes on Camp" in *A Susan Sontag Reader.* (London and New York: Penguin Books,1983), p. s106

Chronology

Jōmon Period	10,500–400 B.C.E.
Yayoi Period	400 B.C.E.–c. 300 C.E.
Kofun Period	c. 300–c. 600
Asuka Period	538–645
Nara Period	710–794
Heian Period	794–1185
Kamakura Period	1185–1333
Nanbokuchô Period	1333–1392
Muromachi Period	1392–1573
Momoyama Period	1573–1615
Edo Period	1615–1868
Meiji Period	1868–1912
Taisho Period	1912–1926
Shōwa Period	1926–1989

CATALOGUE

ANCIENT TIMES

古代 *Kodai*

Ancient Times

Kodai no bi

"[Ancient Japanese] earthenware exudes the smell of Japanese soil and groans under its weight. So robust and relentless—it is tense because it is holding back its explosive energy. Its beauty is almost terrifying—I sense the resonance of an extraordinarily vital rhythm that echoes in the bottom of my stomach. I feel that I can finally stretch my legs, excited with my discovery of the hidden pulse of the nation."

Okamoto Tarō, "What is Tradition?" (1963)[1]

IN THE CANON OF JAPANESE AESTHETICS, *kodai*, literally "ancient times," is the most deeply evocative of concepts. It refers to the prehistoric Jōmon, Yayoi, and Kofun periods that span the millennia of Japanese culture prior to the introduction of Buddhism and continental civilization in the mid-sixth century. It conjures up an agrarian arcadia of the ancient past that precedes written language, state administration, urban design, and all of the other imports from Korea and China that were assimilated and synthesized into traditional Japanese culture.

Free of the moral strictures, along with notions of immortality, that were the purview of imported Buddhism, *kodai* is focused on the spirit of life—fertility and purity. It is a sensitivity that invokes native gods *(kami)* to control the unknown forces of nature and tame them into an order favorable for the vital cycle of rice growing. The great native chronicles of early Japan, *Records of Ancient Matters (Kojiki)* and *Chronicles of Japan (Nihongi)*, compiled in the eighth century C.E., describe the founding of the imperial line by divinities closely associated with natural phenomena—gods and goddesses of the sun, mountains, and sea. It is this supernatural world of shaminist gods and ancient ancestry that the culture of Ancient Times calls to mind. Perpetuated today by the practice of Shinto, "the way of the gods," the ancient *kami* and their *kodai* spirit are revered in shrines all over the country and celebrated, even in the smallest villages, by seasonal festivals *(matsuri)*.

Archaeological excavations of Jōmon (c. 10,000–400 B.C.E.) and Yayoi (400 B.C.E.–300 C.E.) settlements have yielded evidence that a distinct Japanese sense of design, independent of mainland migratory influences, was long established on the Japanese archipelago. The adoption of rice agricultural technology in c. 350 B.C.E created the need for iron-edged spades and hoes, and also saw the production of such utilitarian objects as wooden containers, loom parts, pestles, combs, and ceramic vessels for grain storage. Jars for burial were also common, along with such ceremonial bronzes as daggers and bells. With the development of agrarian culture, the populace was rendered into commoner and elite classes with powerful chiefs emerging, able to command large communities of farmers and artisans. The large mounded tombs built for these leaders mark the beginning of the Kofun period (258–646 C.E.), when the Japanese state was formed.

The culture of Japan's deep past has fascinated important twentieth-century artists and writers from Yanagita Kunio (1875–1962), founder of Japanese folklore studies, to the painter and essayist, Okamoto Tarō (1911–1995). In Okamoto's 1963 essay, "What is Tradition?" he reclaims possession of a native Japanese "primitivism" seen in the form and decoration of recently excavated pots. The stone tools of powerful, abstract form, bold ceramic burial vessels, and fantastic funerary bracelets selected here (Plates 1–6) under the rubric of Ancient Times share the aesthetic of ritual magic and purity that was celebrated and codified by these and other modern Japanese intellectuals.

1. Okamoto Tarō, "Dento-wa nani ka?" (What is Tradition?). Originally published in 1963; translated by Reiko Tomii in Alexandra Munroe, *Japanese Art After 1945: Scream Against the Sky* (Harry N. Abrams, 1994), p. 382.

PLATE 1
Hoe-shaped Bracelet

Kofun period, late 3rd-4th century C.E.
Green steatite
Length: 16 cm
The Metropolitan Museum of Art, The Harry G.C. Packard
Collection of Asian Art, Gift of Harry G.C. Packard, and
Purchase, Fletcher, Rogers, Harris Brisbane Dick, and
Louis V. Bell Funds, Joseph Pulitzer bequest, and the
Annenberg Fund Inc. Gift, 1975 (1975.268.387)

Shell bracelets adorn the lower arms of a small
number of skeletons found in shell-mound burials
from as early as the Early Jōmon period (c. 5000–
3000 B.C.E.). Earrings and anklets appear in burials
from later centuries and by the end of the Jōmon
period, or the first millennium B.C.E., about thirty
percent of the skeletons in larger shell-mounds have
body ornaments. Yayoi-period bracelets were also of
shell and occasionally of bronze, but in the Kofun
period these were replaced with stone bracelets
modeled after the shell types. From the beginning
they must have been status symbols, originally for
both men and women, but later primarily for women.

The most striking were described by Edo-period
writers as "hoe-shaped" (*kuwagata-ishi*) because of
their blade-like projection. The first stone available
for such ornaments was jasper (*hekigyoku*) from the
Izumo area or green tuff from the Hokuriku region,
both on the Japan Sea side, but by far the largest
numbers are copies of these in talc or steatite
(*kasseki*). Most were probably fashioned in local
workshops in the Kinki region (Kyoto, Nara, Osaka,
and immediate vicinity). During the Yayoi period
(300 B.C.E.–250 C.E.) bracelets made of a large
gohōra shell (*Strombus latissimus*), the heaviest of
the tropical and semitropical Indo-Pacific *Strombus*
genus, cut lengthwise. Yayoi skeletons in several
sites in southwest Japan have them on lower
arms—one male in a jar burial has fourteen on the
right arm—but since in most cases the hole is only
large enough for a juvenile hand either they had to
have been worn during an individual's lifetime or slid
over a hand at the time of secondary burial. (Such
secondary burials, or permanent internment of
bones that have been cleaned in jars, sarchophagi,
or family mausoleums, are recorded throughout the
Jōmon period.) Bracelets are not found on arms in
the Kofun period (250–550 C.E.), but were
arranged around the coffin or stacked fairly near
the head. [E.K.]

PLATE 2
Wheel-shaped Bracelet

Early Kofun period, late 3rd–early 4th century C.E.
Steatite
1.3 x 8.9 cm
The Metropolitan Museum of Art, The Harry G. C. Packard
Collection of Asian Art, Gift of Harry G. C. Packard, and
Purchase, Fletcher, Rogers, Harris Brisbane Dick, and Louis
V. Bell Funds, Joseph Pulitzer Bequest, and the Annenberg
Fund Inc. Gift, 1975 (1975.268.388)

Among the three types of bracelets copied from
shells, the so-called wheel-shaped (*sharin-seki*) was the
most popular. They resemble a sword guard in shape,
but are ribbed to reproduce the appearance of their
bivalve models. In the large keyhole-shaped
Shimanoyama tomb in Nara prefecture, opened in
1996, eighty bracelets among the one hundred and
forty that lined the outside of the coffin were of this
type. Although the human remains had disappeared,
the grave goods indicate that the occupant of this
tomb was a female shaman. Three bronze mirrors lay
near the head of the deceased, long beads that had
once formed a diadem were scattered above the
head, and three strands of beads lay at the neck. The
tomb had no iron swords, which are usually believed
to accompany male burials.

From other examples there is now strong indication
that such collections of bracelets were by this time
the mark of women who ranked high in the political
hierarchy. Many early tombs in the Kinki region contain
them. The Kushiyama tomb, also in Nara prefecture,
yielded 252 bracelets. During the third and fourth
centuries the most prominent chieftains exercised
indivisible secular and religious power, but as the
ancient Yamato state evolved politically and became
more centralized, the authority tended to be sepa-
rated between the ruler and his wife. Grave goods
became more secular and military in nature and stone
bracelets went out of style. [E.K.]

PLATE 3
Polished Ax

Late Jōmon period, c. 2000–1000 B.C.E.
Serpentine
Length: 15.9 cm
The Metropolitan Museum of Art, The Harry G. C. Packard
Collection of Asian Art, Gift of Harry G. C. Packard, and
Purchase, Fletcher, Rogers, Harris Brisbane Dick, and Louis
V. Bell Funds, Joseph Pulitzer Bequest, and the Annenberg
Fund Inc. Gift, 1975 (1975.268.265)

A small number of ground and polished axes had
supplemented the tool kit from Early Jōmon times, but
they increased in popularity from Late Jōmon and
continued into the Yayoi period, when a continental
bronze type of ax was reproduced in stone. Serpen-

tine (*jamon-seki*) is widely available throughout the country except were volcanic ash has created plains. Sturdy chipped tools of such stone as hard slate, Greywacke sandstone, quartz schist, and andesite did double duty as axes and adzes for tree cutting and ground digging, but most polished axes show little evidence of heavy use. This blade has only miniscule nicks. An occasional example in the late stages of the Jōmon period might be as small as one inch in length, suggesting that it had undergone several stages of grinding to keep the blade smooth.

The regular chipped axes tend to be made of local stone or, for the Kantō Plain (the hinterland of Tokyo), stone brought from the central mountains, but polished axes were apparently made in fewer places and became valuable trade items. In view of the quality of the stone, the fine satiny finish, the relatively dull blade, and the limited functional use, many may have been status symbols, votive objects, or intended primarily as burial goods.   [E.K.]

PLATE 4
Horned and Stemmed Ax
Mid-late Yayoi period, 1st–3rd century C.E.
Basalt
Length: 25.4 cm
The Metropolitan Museum of Art, ahe Harry G. C. Packard Collection of Asian Art, Gift of Harry G. C. Packard, and Purchase, Fletcher, Rogers, Harris Brisbane Dick, and Louis V. Bell Funds, Joseph Pulitzer Bequest, and the Annenberg Fund Inc. Gift, 1975 (1975.268.264)

This unusual object is a much elaborated form of a tool known as *yūkaku-sekifu*, literally "horned ax." The functional examples have a rounded blade, a pair of more or less triangular projections in the middle, and a rounded or oval stem at the other end. The middle "horns" were probably intended to provide knobs for lashing the tool to its wooden handle. The sides of the stem of the implement are slightly squared off.

Horned axes were once looked on as products of the late Jōmon culture in the north, but with increased excavations of Yayoi sites in the southern Tōhoku region, their context and distribution are now clear. Their basalt is of volcanic origin, which prehistoric people collected near mounts Zao and Bandai in the Nasu Volcanic Belt. Slight damage to the blade indicates that it saw only moderate practical use. As a fine piece, it probably served out its above-ground life as a ceremonial object, an item of prestige and power.   [E.K.]

PLATE 5
Stand with Attached Miniature Vessels
Attributed to late Kofun period, 6th–7th century C.E.
Sue ware; gray stoneware with natural-ash glaze
Height: 16.5 cm
Brooklyn Museum of Art, Gift of Mrs. Albert H. Clayburgh in memory of her mother, Mrs. E. Evelyn Dorr (66.33)

Sue ware was a sophisticated ceramic form introduced from south Korea during the fifth century. More demand for its type led to the use of the pottery wheel, and vessels were fired at a high temperature in fairly primitive step kilns. Since Haji earthenware, a direct descendant of Yayoi pottery, already existed

for domestic use, Sue became a major component of grave goods. It is not unusual for a tomb to yield scores of Sue pieces. Only later was it converted to chiefly household use.

The name comes from Sue-mura, an area in Osaka prefecture where it was thought the ware was first made. There is some question today whether this actually occurred there, but more than 600 kilns were at some time in operation at Sue-mura and, as the first major production center, pottery was shipped from there to places hundreds of miles away. Only after good ceramic clay became scarce in this area around the tenth century did production slacken and potters gave up the trade or moved elsewhere. Very little pottery was made there after that time.

Vessels like this were essentially stands to support rows of little jars and plates, which more or less alternate with each other on some very late examples from the Tokyo area. They were often attached to the shoulder or were sometimes set into large plates or bowls. The shoulders of some tall pedestalled vessels in the Kansai and eastern Inland Sea region may also bear rather crudely made human figures, animals, and birds. The little jars added to the capacity of vessels of this type, which probably held sake as libations to the dead. [E.K.]

PLATE 6
Jar
Middle Yayoi period, c. 1st century C.E.
Earthenware with smoke blackening, brushed surface and appliqué buttons
27.7 x 15.8 cm
Brooklyn Museum of Art, Gift of Carl H. De Silver, by exchange and the Oriental Art Acquisitions Fund (74.26.1)

With the introduction of metal objects and rice agriculture by the beginning of the Yayoi period, pottery became more specialized in shape and use, at first in varieties of cooking and storage pots. The former are identified by a wide mouth and the latter by a narrowed neck and smaller mouth, which together made it convenient to tie on a cover of wicker or some other material. Burial jars, used exclusively for human remains (sometimes accompanied by a few grave goods) and normally in secondary burials, begin to appear, and by the Middle Yayoi period ceremonial vessels and stands completed the inventory. In contrast to the rich and imaginative decoration on most Jōmon pots, Yayoi pots have more of a functional uniformity and, if decorated at all, are most often only brushed, combed, or painted red. However, in the Kinki region, where there was a flourishing woodworking business, many pots have scratched and painted geometric designs based on floral patterns, and some have little primitive sketches of animals, people, and storage buildings on the shoulder or side. Farther north, vessels acquired fine bands of cord-marking, borrowed from the old Jōmon tradition. Yayoi vessels are often extremely attractive in their sheer simplicity and neat workmanship. The globularity of this storage vessel, rather short neck, mouth and lip profile are Kansai region characteristics. Yayoi pots found in the Tokyo region often bear little clay discs in short rows. [E.K.]

PLATE 1
Hoe-shaped Bracelet
Kofun period, late 3rd–4th century C.E.
The Metropolitan Museum of Art

PLATE 2
Wheel-shaped Bracelet
Early Kofun period, late 3rd–early 4th century C.E.
The Metropolitan Museum of Art

PLATE 3
Polished Ax
Late Jōmon period, c. 2000–1000 B.C.E.
The Metropolitan Museum of Art

PLATE 4
Horned and Stemmed Ax
Mid-late Yayoi period, 1st–3rd century C.E.
The Metropolitan Museum of Art

PLATE 5
Stand with Attached Miniature Vessels
Attributed to late Kofun period, 6th–7th century C.E.
Brooklyn Museum of Art

PLATE 6
Jar
Middle Yayoi period, c. 1st century C.E.
Brooklyn Museum of Art

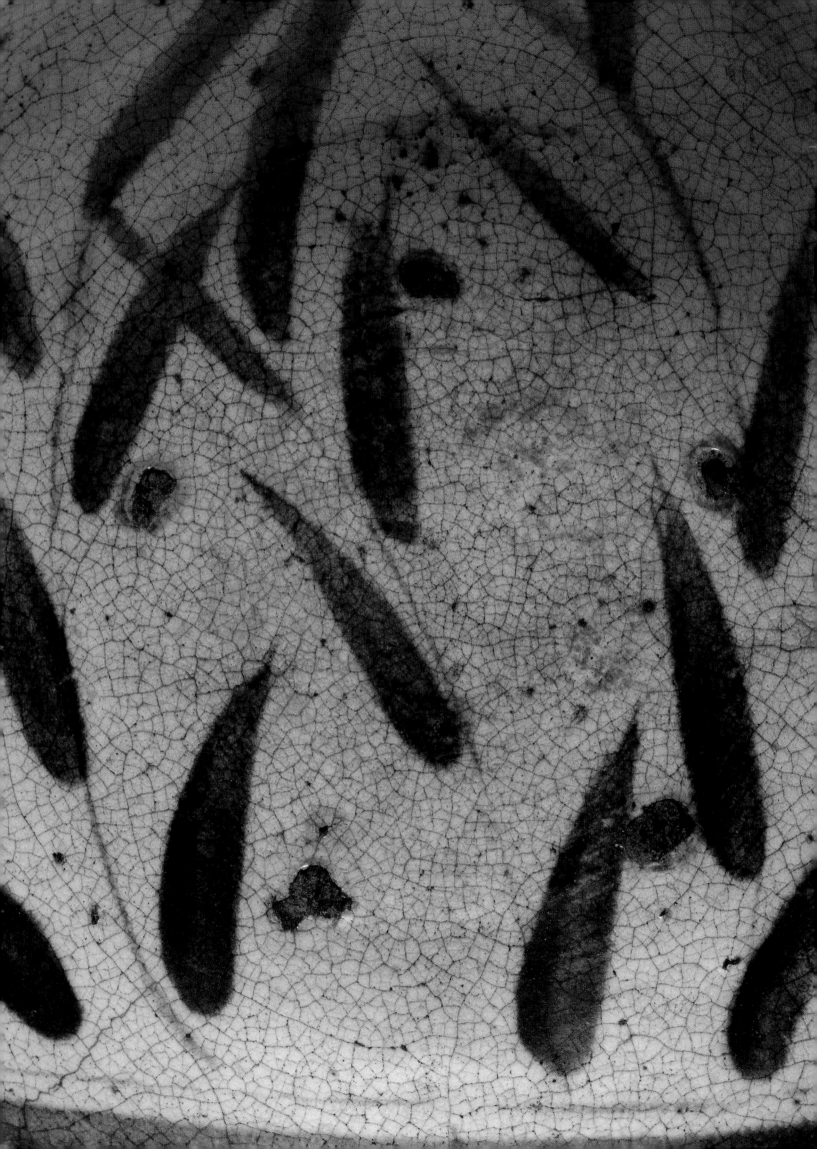

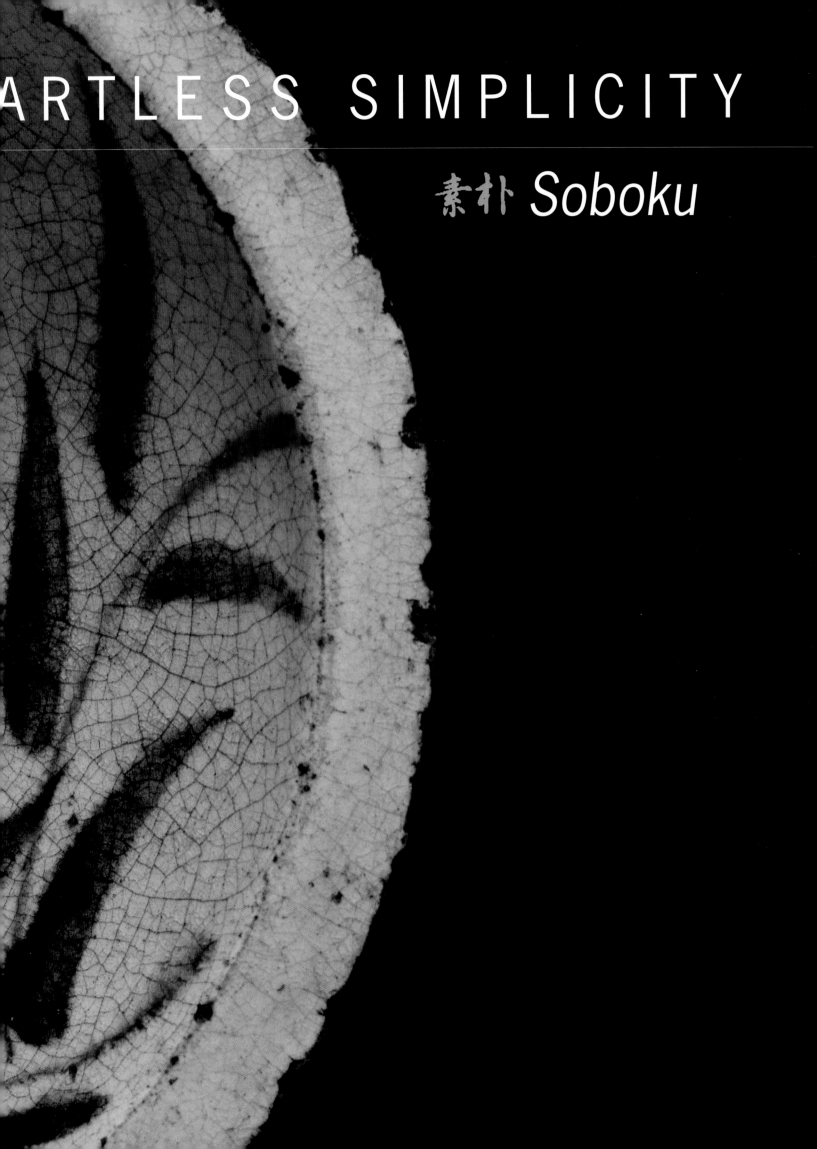

ARTLESS SIMPLICITY

素朴 *Soboku*

Artless Simplicity

Soboku

The special quality of beauty in crafts is that it is a beauty of intimacy. Since the articles are to be lived with every day, this quality of intimacy is a natural requirement. Such beauty establishes a world of grace and feeling. It is significant that in speaking of craft objects, people use terms such as savor and style. The beauty of such objects is not so much of the noble, the huge, or the lofty as a beauty of the warm and familiar. Here one may detect a striking difference between the crafts and the arts. People hang their pictures high up on walls, but they place their objects for everyday use close to them and take them in their hands.

Yanagi Sōetsu, *The Unknown Craftsman* (c. 1950)[1]

SOBOKU, WHICH MEANS SIMPLE, unsophisticated, and artless, applies to the traditional crafts that evolved in the countryside of Japan—objects that were made of natural materials and intended for everyday, practical use in the rustic life of common Japanese. The forms of these tools and vessels, and the methods of their design and manufacture, developed over centuries, becoming more or less standardized by the early Edo period (1615–1868). With the advent of industrialization, the survival of traditional Japanese crafts and the beauty of their inherent artlessness was threatened. Such objects were simply taken for granted and attracted little attention until the early part of the twentieth century when their aesthetic qualities were recognized and articulated by collector and arts activist Yanagi Sōetsu (1889–1961), founder of the Japanese folk art (*mingei*) movement and author of the classic book, *The Unknown Craftsman*, which ascribes the purest form of Japanese aesthetics to those anonymous artisans who produced well-designed utilitarian objects.

Yanagi's promotion of *mingei* (literally, people's art) was linked to the appreciation of *soboku* taste—one that is stripped of artifice or intellectual contrivance. In his book, he argues convincingly that the dichotomy of seeing and knowing was a major barrier to the understanding of beauty. He anticipates the criticism that, "intuitive perception of beauty is incomplete without learning," by pointing out that, "to be unable to *see* beauty properly is to lack the basic foundation for any aesthetic understanding." To *see* an object is to go directly to its core—the essence of its beauty—while factual and intellectual discrimination only serves to skirt the periphery. He quotes Socrates and Aquinas to illustrate that his philosophy is neither new nor a solely Asian construct, but one that has universal application.

Borrowing from Zen ideals, Yanagi explains that the relativist polarity of beauty and ugliness is a duality waiting to trap any aesthete. He explains that, "from the Buddhist's point of view, the 'beauty' that simply stands opposed to 'ugliness' is not true beauty…True beauty exists in the realm where there is no distinction between the beautiful and the ugly." Objects of rustic simplicity, made with a single purpose in mind, may be the opposite of gorgeous ethos described in the taste *Karei* but are, in Yanagi's eyes, the essence of beauty.

Yanagi praises the unknown craftsmen of China, Korea, and Japan for their lack of intention to make "art." Traditional artisans developed their skills by self-reliant doing (*jiriki*), not by thinking, so that with practice, spontaneous and superb creation became second nature. *Tariki,* which connotes detachment, "it is not I who am doing this," is another mark of the artisan and indicates a surrender to an external, almost supernatural power. The endless repetition, without the chance of even a second of hesitation, led to a free dexterity and gesturality. From such spontaneity, products of artistic quality were born rather than made.

The objects gathered here as examples of Artless Simplicity are domestic items that were traditionally used in every farmer's household—kettle hooks hewn from trunks of wood (Plate 10), baskets for winnowing grain (Plate 21), ceramic jars for storage (Plates 26, 27), indigo cotton textiles for warmth and durability (Plate 25). These objects show little or no surface decoration beyond the natural patina of their rustic material, and their form is an efficient expression of their function. They were appreciated from one generation to the next for the comfort of their design and have come to be appreciated by aesthetes as expressions of *soboku*, tools whose essential forms and plain decoration evoke an appealing authenticity.

1. Yanagi Sōetsu, *The Unknown Craftsman: A Japanese Insight into Beauty.* Adapted by Bernard Leach. (Tokyo and New York: Kodansha International, 1972), p. 198. This anthology is drawn from writings by Yanagi that were originally published in Japanese, c. 1940–1955.

PLATE 7
Spouted Bowl
Edo period, 18th century
Wajima ware; red lacquer
21 x 36 x 26 cm
Jeffrey Montgomery Collection (MC 180)

Bowls with long, open spouts (*kataguchi)* were used for pouring sake. Both the large size and felicitous red color suggest that this bowl may have been designed for wedding ceremonies. This type of high-quality lacquer was made at Wajima (on the Noto Peninsula of Honshu, Japan's main island) where craftsmen continue to work today. Earlier Wajima lacquer like this piece tends to be of a single color, usually red or black; more modern works of the late nineteenth and twentieth centuries often have incised decorations and the application of gold leaf.

The process of making lacquer wares is complex and usually involves a team of craftsmen, each responsible for one stage of production. The basic form is carved from wood on which layers of primer material—strips of lacquer-soaked fabric—are applied. Undercoats of burned earth mixed with rice paste and lacquer are layered on before the piece is given its surface finish.   [M.D.]

PLATE 8
Kneading Basin
Edo period, 19th century
Paulownia wood
13 x 80 cm
Jeffrey Montgomery Collection (MC 217)

A large basin such as this *kone-bachi* was most likely used for drying rice cakes (*mochi*). Cooked rice was pounded to a fine paste in a mortar, especially at the New Year when festive dishes based on rice cakes are traditional. The rice paste would be spread out on a platter like this to dry before being cut into usable portions.

Paulownia wood, which has the desirable property of expanding or contracting with fluctuations in humidity, rarely splits and so was a good choice for this object. The wood is rather soft, revealing chisel marks and small nicks of use that add interest to the surface.   [M.D.]

PLATE 9
Fulling Mallet and Block
Edo period, 19th century
Wood
Mallet: 23 x 11 cm; block: 14.5 x 24 cm
Jeffery Montgomery Collection (MC 218.1-.2)

The robust design of this wooden mallet and block is well suited to its function, "fulling," or beating soaked, newly woven cloth to soften it. The mark on the base of the mallet may identify the owner: fulling cloth was a group activity and each woman brought similar tools, making it useful to differentiate who owned which set. Splits in the wood suggest that this object has seen long wear and handling and add to its character.   [M.D.]

PLATE 10
Kettle Hanger
Late Edo-early Meiji period, 19th century
Zelkova wood
47 x 40 x 20.5 cm
Jeffrey Montgomery Collection (MC 212)

An assemblage consisting of a vertical wooden support (*jizai-gake*) and hook (*jizai-kagi*) was used to suspend cooking vessels from a rafter over the floor hearth in a traditional farmhouse. Family members gathered at the hearth, where guests were entertained, and so the *jizai* assemblage occupied a prominent place. The central square hearth was the only part of the house kept consistently warm during the winter, and a kettle of water was kept at the boil for making a constant supply of tea.

The simple shape of the *jizai-kagi* is enhanced by the rich color and decorative grain of the solid piece of expensive zelkova (*keyaki*) wood from which it is made. A transverse groove has been worn into this *jizai-kagi* by the rope suspending the kettle.   [M.D.]

PLATE 11
Kettle Hanger Adjusters
Late Edo-early Meiji period, 19th century
Zelkova wood
Left: 9.5 x 30.3 x 6 cm
Right: 12.5 x 37.5 x 6 cm
Jeffrey Montgomery Collection (MC 124.1-.2)

Yokogi were used to adjust the length of a pot hanger to bring a cooking vessel closer to or further from the fire. Because the hearth was the center of family life in a traditional Japanese farmhouse, the *yokogi* would be a prominent element of a home's décor, in full view of family members and guests. Subjects were carved in auspicious forms; carp or sea bream fish, which had lucky connotations, were particularly favored. The simple, clean shapes of these *yokogi* are in the form of the brush-written character *ichi*, the number one, which may have been chosen because this character was part of the owner's name, Yamaichi, for instance.   [M.D.]

PLATE 12
Cooking Vessel
Edo period, 19th century
Cast iron, red lacquer lid
9 x 26.3 cm
Jeffrey Montgomery Collection (MC 199)

This cast-iron casserole stands on three metal feet, molded onto its bottom, that lifted it above the hot ashes in the hearth. Although it is well suited for the everyday purpose of cooking, its design is refined, with four indentations hinting at the cross-section of a pumpkin. The red lacquer lid contrasts with the matte black iron pot, which has two elegant handles for lifting. Communally eaten dishes—such as stews —were both cooked and served from casseroles like this.   [M.D.]

PLATE 13
Tea Kettle
Meiji period, late 19th century
Cast iron, bronze lid ring
20 x 18 cm
Jeffrey Montgomery Collection (MC 437)

This iron tea kettle is cast as a hemisphere sur-mounted by a half cube. Its base is shaped to stand easily on a trivet set in the burning charcoal of a hearth. The interlocking elements are beautifully balanced and could be symbolically representative of Heaven and Earth. Small, round indentations on the hemispherical shoulder of the kettle show an arrangement similar to that of the Great Bear constellation, which may be another element in this symbolic scheme.   [M.D.]

PLATE 14
Ship's Sake Container
Momoyama period, 16th–17th century
Bizen ware; stoneware with natural-ash glaze
30 x 28 cm
Jeffrey Montgomery Collection (MC 702)

The Bizen complex of kilns has been making stoneware pottery of a characteristic reddish color since the early medieval period. Bizen clay requires long firing in the kiln to fuse into stoneware and does not lend itself to the application of glazes, but the natural effects caused by molten ash in the kiln are appreciated. A common technique in Bizen during the Momoyama period was to shelter the clay vessel beneath an inverted dish before firing in the kiln. This prevented falling ash from covering the surface and created a different atmosphere under the dish so that the clay would fire to a different color.

Funadokkuri, used to transport sake on the ships that plied coastal waters, are shaped with a wide bottom that can withstand rough motion without falling over. In this masterpiece, the spectacular effects of Bizen kiln-stacking techniques have created a dark red matte color on the neck and mouth; the body, which was exposed, is decorated with drips of natural ash glaze like melted caramel. [M.D.]

PLATE 15
Sake Bottle
Edo period, 19th century
Fujina ware; glazed stoneware with iron-oxide and white ash glaze
Height: 25 cm
Jeffrey Montgomery Collection (MC 481)

The Fujina kilns were established during the mid-Edo period and are located on the shore of Lake Shinji near Matsue on the Japan Sea coast. This sturdy sake bottle in the shape and color of an eggplant has an iron glaze applied to the body. Some of the whitish glaze around the shoulder, neck, and mouth has dripped, making a pleasing abstract pattern. [M.D.]

PLATE 16
Sake Bottle
Late Momoyama-early Edo period, 17th century
Bizen ware; stoneware
Height: 29 cm
Victor and Takako Hauge Collection

The complex of Bizen kilns, located on the Inland Sea between Himeji and Okayama, still produces unglazed ceramic wares of a characteristic red color. Bizen clay, which is dug up from a meter or so underneath rice paddy fields, has a very fine texture that tends to shrink during firing and is not amenable to glazes. The plastic quality of Bizen clay allows for very fine potting, and the unusually long firing, up to twelve days, yields an extremely hard and durable stoneware that is much admired. The high iron content is responsible for the deep red color. Other surface effects were caused by natural molten ash in the kiln, or the use of straw or stacking techniques to create different atmospheres during firing that protected some pieces from ash and produced different colors.

The spout of this generously sized sake bottle tilted a little during the firing: this off-kilter element expresses the unassuming nature of *soboku* taste and gives this piece great character.   [M.D.]

PLATE 17
Spouted Beaker
Edo period, 17th century
Hizen ware, Karatsu type; glazed stoneware
9.3 x 17.8 cm
Museum of Fine Arts, Boston, Morse Collection, Gift by
Contribution (92.3105)

The Karatsu kilns, located in the north of Kyushu,
the westernmost of the four main Japanese islands,
were influenced by Korean potters who immigrated
after Japanese military incursions on the peninsula
at the end of the sixteenth century. Although a
variety of wares were produced, those most
associated with Karatsu are known as painted
Karatsu (e-Karatsu) and typically show freely drawn
designs in underglaze iron on a grayish brown body.

This pouring vessel shows the chips and abrasion of
everyday use in a farmhouse kitchen. The simple
decoration of this piece complements the satisfying
round form.   [M.D.]

PLATE 18
Soba Cups
Edo period, 18th century
Arita ware; glazed porcelain
Height of each approximately 6.6 cm
Brooklyn Museum of Art, Gift of Greg and Natalie Fitz-
Gerald (1996.1.1-5)

The Arita kilns in northern Kyushu (southwestern
Japan) were established by immigrant Korean
potters who introduced the techniques of making
porcelain. Porcelain differs from stoneware in that it
has a characteristic white body made from kaolin
clay that is fired to a temperature above 1300
degrees Centigrade. The result is a very hard
ceramic that is waterproof even when unglazed and
will ring like a bell when struck.

Most Arita porcelains are decorated with underglaze
painting in cobalt blue, and many with overglaze
colored enamels. This set of cups (soba-chokko),
used to hold a sauce for dipping buckwheat
noodles, is rare because it has no decoration. The
pure forms and plain white color can be appreciated
as an expression of soboku taste.   [M.D.]

PLATE 19
Large Dish
Edo period, 17th century
Yatsushiro ware; glazed stoneware with incised design
11.5 x 42 cm
Jeffrey Montgomery Collection (MC 330)

The Yatsushiro kilns in western Kyushu near
Kumamoto were most likely established by Korean
potters, who had arrived in the early seventeenth
century after military incursions led by the Shogun
Toyotomi Hideyoshi (1585–98). Kyushu ceramic
wares are divided into "dark" wares—stoneware
made with a body of dark-colored clay—and "white"

porcelain wares made with a fine kaolin clay. Many
pottery centers throughout the island made "dark"
wares for use in local farmhouse kitchens. "White"
porcelains were mainly made in Hizen province in the
northwest for local, upper-class customers and for
export via the Dutch East Indies Company, which was
permitted to trade from the island of Deshima at
Nagasaki.

Using the simple materials that were locally
available, potters showed resourceful ingenuity in
decorating their pots to make them more attractive.
This dish has been embellished with wavy lines
carved into the body and a light feldspathic glaze
splashed to create an effect that is artless and
gestural. Because this large dish is thin walled and
fragile, it is extraordinary that it has survived three
centuries of use in perfect condition.   [M.D.]

PLATE 20
Basket
Late Edo–early Meiji period, 19th century
Birch bark, rope with bone toggle
19.3 x 17.5 x 10.5 cm
Jeffrey Montgomery Collection (MC 226)

Baskets made of birch bark instead of bamboo are
usually found in the mountainous areas of Japan
such as Gifu Prefecture where this example
originated; in Akita Prefecture (northern Honshu)
cherry tree bark is used for the same purpose.
Because of its compact size it can be presumed
that this basket was used as a lunch container;
larger baskets were used as backpacks or panniers.
Both the lid and the box have small loops around the
sides for a cord to pass through and the bone
toggle can be pushed down the cord to keep the lid
in place.   [M.D]

PLATE 21
Winnower
Late Meiji-early Taisho period, 20th century
Woven split bamboo
20 x 53 x 65 cm
Jeffrey Montgomery Collection (MC 229)

The wide shape of this basket made it suitable for
winnowing rice—tossing the threshed grains into the
air to allow the breeze to carry off the chaff—a
process that in recent decades has been done by
machine. This example comes from Tokushima
Prefecture at the eastern end of Shikoku Island.
Even though the object was made for hard work, its
creator was inspired to weave in strips of a lighter-
colored bamboo to make a simple but attractive
cross-pattern.   [M.D.]

PLATE 22
Dish

Edo period, 18th–19th century
Seto ware; glazed stoneware, iron-oxide and cobalt-blue design
6.8 x 27 cm
Jeffrey Montgomery Collection (MC 425)

Stoneware plates and dishes (*ishizara*) made at the Seto complex of kilns (near Nagoya) during the late Edo period are prized for their appealing designs, which use motifs inspired by the natural world. They were produced in large quantities, and the quickly applied decoration demonstrates the *soboku* taste of artless gesturality that is commonly attributed to folk art.

Large pieces of *ishizara* like this were used for serving food in large country households, restaurants, and hostelries for travelers. Here the potter has decorated the surface with a design of dwarf bamboo brushed in iron-oxide brown and cobalt blue under a clear glaze.   [M.D.]

PLATE 23
Oil Dish

Edo period, 18th–19th century
Seto ware; glazed stoneware, iron-oxide design and copper glaze
Diameter: 23 cm
Jeffrey Montgomery Collection (MC 336)

Small, flat stoneware plates were placed at the bottom of a cylindrical paper lantern (*andon*) to catch any drips of oil or wax from the candle or lamp. This example of such a receptacle has been partially dipped in a deep-green glaze that is also more associated with the Oribe wares of the nearby Mino kilns. The three roundels painted in underglaze iron oxide depict crosscut sections of charcoal—an everyday sight for Japanese people before the modern era; this juxtaposition of the decorative and the mundane is typical of the *soboku* aesthetic. [M.D.]

PLATE 24
Travel Cape

Edo period, 19th century
Cotton, indigo, paper interlining
100 x 243 cm
Jeffrey Montgomery Collection (MC 700)

Cone-shaped capes such as this one were likely adapted from a style worn by Dutch traders and Portuguese missionary priests living and working in Japan in the late sixteenth century. Called *bozu-gappa*, a compound formed from the Japanese character for "priest" and the Japanese transliteration of "cape" in Portuguese, such capes were initially used only by Japan's military elite. By the eighteenth century, people of all social classes were wearing these capes in Japan.

These travel cloaks were typically made of two layers of thick cotton fabric, commonly in indigo blue with white patterns rendered in the technique called *kasuri*. Traditionally, before the cloth was woven, threads of the warp or weft or both were resist-dyed by binding them in places where the dye color was not wanted. The *kasuri* pattern, a contrast between the dyed and undyed areas, emerged as the cloth was woven. The bold blue and white *kasuri* design on the outside of this cape appears to be plain woven slats of bamboo. The inside layer is a simple blue and white vertical stripe.   [A.V.A.]

PLATE 25
Overcoat

Meiji period, late 19th century
Cotton, indigo, quilting
139.7 x 113.3 cm
The Metropolitan Museum of Art, Purchase, Mrs. Jackson Burke Gift, 1979 (1979.409)

Sashiko, derived from the Japanese verb *sasu* (to stitch or pierce) and *ko* (small), is a quilting technique used to gather several layers of fabric to create a cloth that is both durable and warm. The technique initially developed out of necessity in rural Japan as a practical means to reinforce or mend well-worn garments. Women traditionally were the makers of *sashiko* coats, and these coats were often included in a woman's dowry.

Indigo was a favorite dye material for rural garments because of its long-lasting color, and resistence to soiling. Indigo-dyed cloth also exudes a distinctive ammonia odor that wards off snakes and insects, granting the wearer protection in the fields.

The stitching patterns on this coat are persimmon flower on the upper and lower body panels; hemp leaf on the sleeve and center of the body panel; and a zigzag pattern son the lapel and collar. Stitching patterns became increasingly important as the craft evolved, and certain designs were often identified with a particular village.   [A.V.A.]

PLATE 26
Storage Jar
Muromachi period, 16th century
Tamba ware; stoneware with natural-ash glaze
49 x 40 cm
Jeffrey Montgomery Collection (MC 136)

Tamba wares have been produced in the Sasayama area of Hyogo Prefecture, west of Kyoto, from early medieval times until the present. The center is one of the so-called six ancient kilns—along with Echizen, Shiga, Bizen, Tokoname, and Seto—that evolved with many others from earlier Sueki and Sanage kilns.

Farmers used such large jars to store rice seed through the winter for planting in the spring. The small flared mouth could be sealed to protect the contents from insects and rodents. These pots, made by the coiled-rope method before being finished on a potter's wheel, were largely undecorated. The comb marks on this piece are probably accidental. The pots were fired in climbing, chambered, wood-burning kilns, and natural wood ash carried by the updraught would melt, forming attractive green drips, which contrast with the warm, reddish-sand color of the body.   [M.D.]

PLATE 27
Storage Jar
Momoyama period, late 16th century
Iga ware; stoneware with natural-ash glaze
30.5 x 22.8 cm
Philadelphia Museum of Art, The John T. Morris Fund and The John D. McIlhenny Fund (1993-66-1)

The Iga kilns are located slightly south of the medieval Shigaraki kilns in present-day Mie Prefecture. Both kilns use clay dug from Lake Biwa, and their wares are often similar. During the Momoyama period the Iga kilns rose in status, however, as they began to produce wares for the tea ceremony under the guidance of leading aesthetes such as Furuta Oribe and Kobori Enshū.

This jar has the sturdy shape and subdued natural ash glaze typical of the form and glaze used for tea storage jars. The flared lip was designed so that a cover could be tied on to protect the contents.   [M.D.]

PLATE 7
Spouted Bowl
Edo period, 18th century
Jeffrey Montgomery Collection

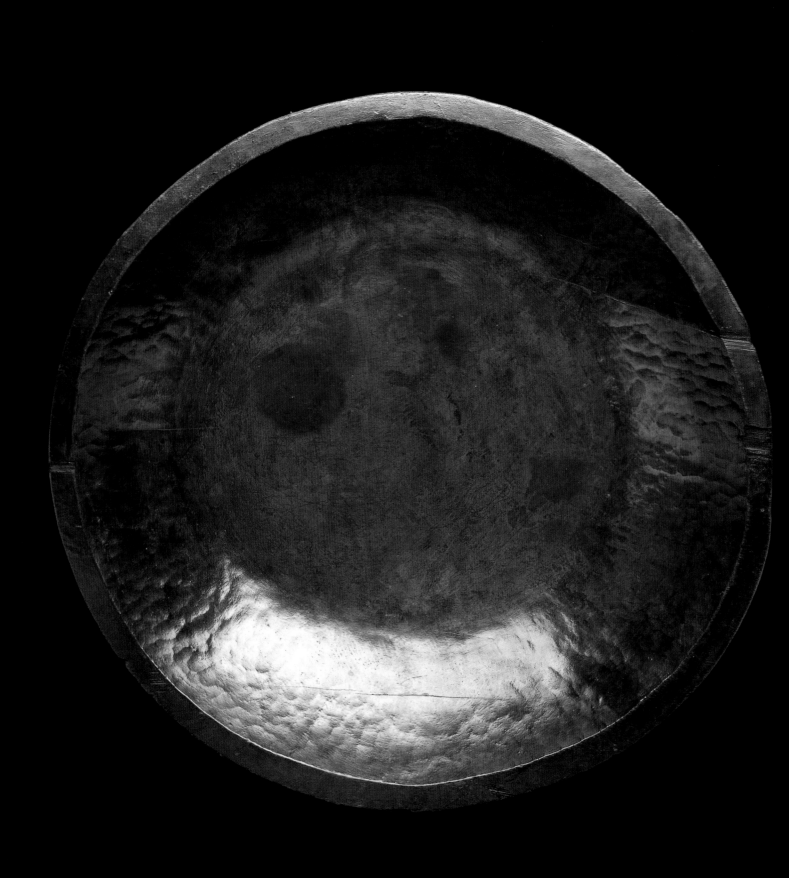

PLATE 8
Kneading Basin
Edo period, 19th century
Jeffrey Montgomery Collection

PLATE 9
Fulling Mallet and Block
Edo period, 19th century
Jeffery Montgomery Collection

PLATE 10
Kettle Hanger
Late Edo–early Meiji period, 19th century
Jeffrey Montgomery Collection

PLATE 11
Kettle Hanger Adjusters
Late Edo-early Meiji period, 19th century
Jeffrey Montgomery Collection

PLATE 12
Cooking Vessel
Edo period, 19th century
Jeffrey Montgomery Collection

PLATE 13
Tea Kettle
Meiji period, late 19th century
Jeffrey Montgomery Collection

PLATE 14
Ship's Sake Container
Momoyama period, 16th–17th century
Jeffrey Montgomery Collection

PLATE 15
Sake Bottle
Edo period, 19th century
Jeffrey Montgomery Collection

PLATE 16
Sake Bottle
Late Momoyama-early Edo period, 17th century
Victor and Takako Hauge Collection

PLATE 17
Spouted Beaker
Edo period, 17th century
Museum of Fine Arts, Boston

PLATE 18
Soba Cups
Edo period, 18th century
Brooklyn Museum of Art

PLATE 19
Large Dish
Edo period, 17th century
Jeffrey Montgomery Collection

PLATE 20
Basket
Late Edo–early Meiji period, 19th century
Jeffrey Montgomery Collection

PLATE 21
Winnower
Late Meiji-early Taisho period, 20th century
Jeffrey Montgomery Collection

PLATE 22
Dish
Edo period, 18th–19th century
Jeffrey Montgomery Collection

PLATE 23
Oil Dish
Edo period, 18th–19th century
Jeffrey Montgomery Collection

PLATE 24
Travel Cape
Edo period, 19th century
Jeffrey Montgomery Collection

PLATE 25
Overcoat
Meiji period, late 19th century
The Metropolitan Museum of Art

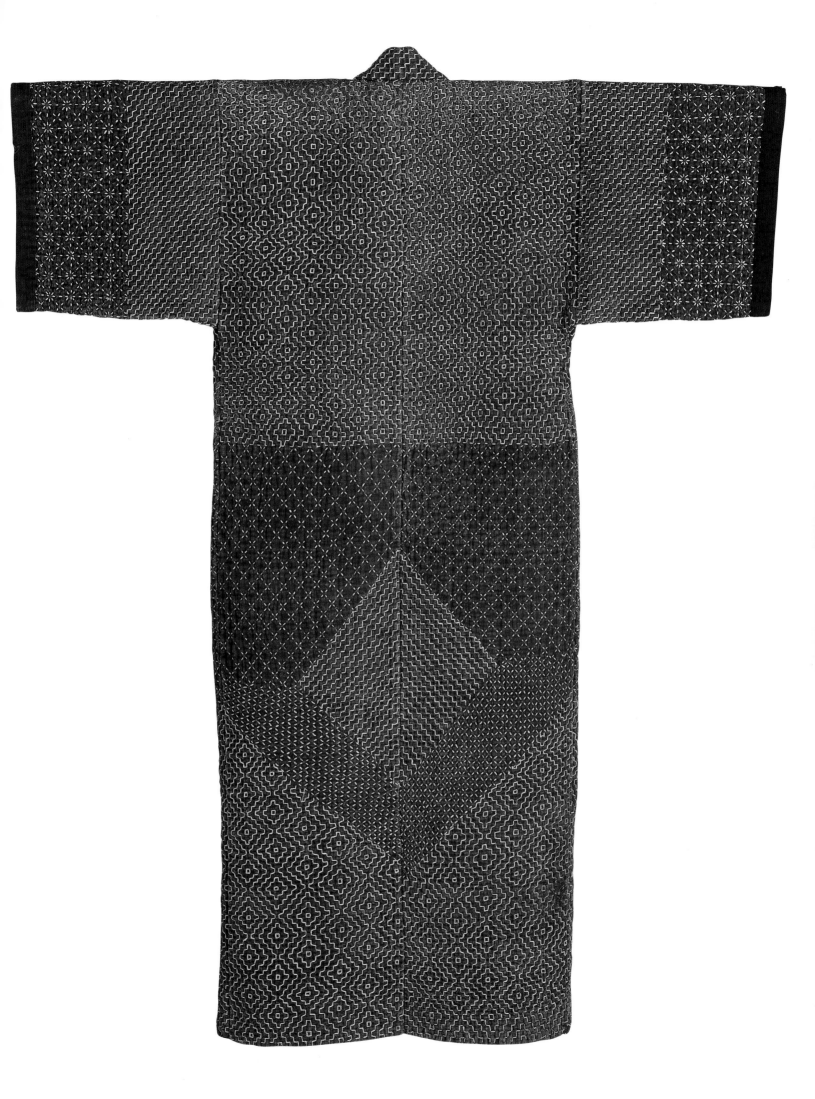

PLATE 26
Storage Jar
Muromachi period, 16th century
Jeffrey Montgomery Collection

PLATE 27
Storage Jar
Momoyama period, late 16th century
Philadelphia Museum of Art

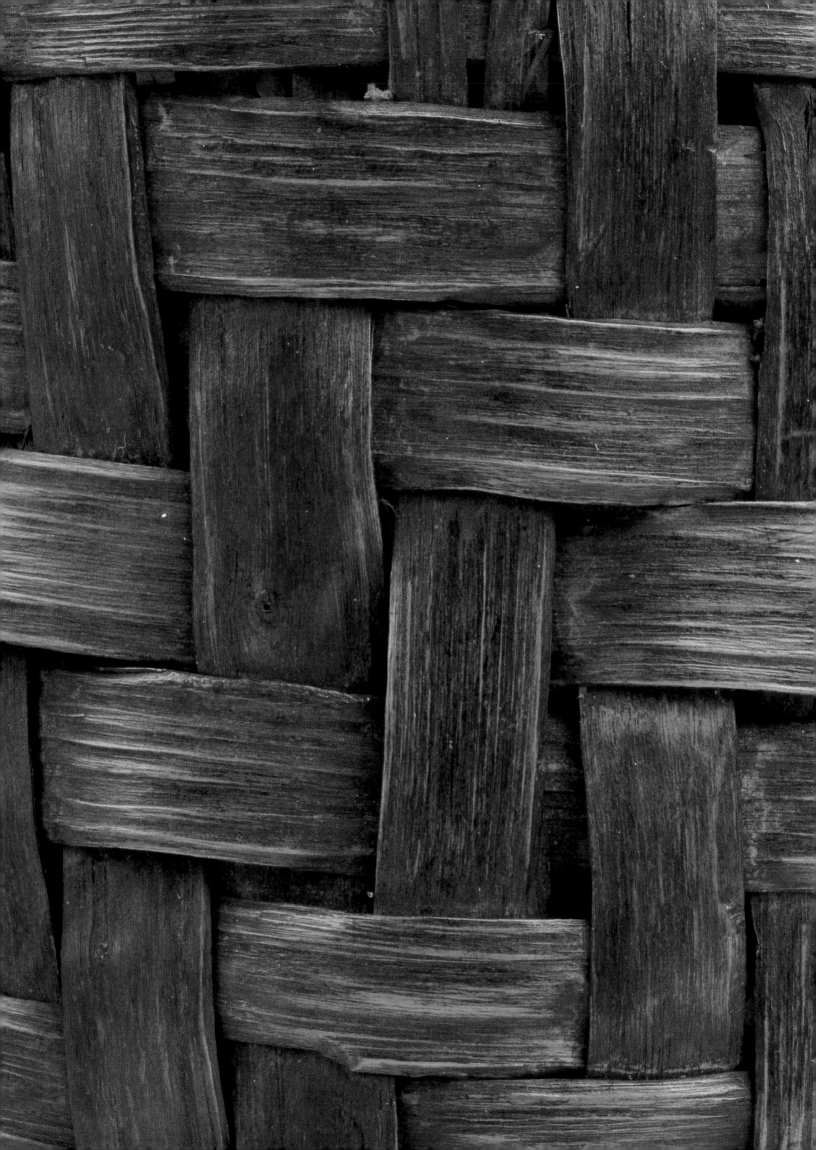

ZEN AUSTERITY

俺 *Wabi*

Zen Austerity

Wabi

To be poor, that is, not to be dependent on things worldly—wealth, power, and reputation—and yet to feel inwardly the presence of something of the highest value, above time and social position: this is what essentially constitutes wabi.

Daisetz T. Suzuki, Zen and Japanese Culture (1959)[1]

WABI IS THE AESTHETIC SENSE most associated with the tea ceremony *(chanoyu)* as codified by Sen no Rikyū (1522–1591) and cultivated by tea masters, Zen monks, and connoisseurs of refined taste in the arts throughout the Edo (1615–1868) and early Meiji periods (1868–1912). Under Rikyū's direction, the *wabi* aesthetic defined the style of architecture, furnishings, and utensils of the tearoom. Literally, *wabi* connotes poverty, the state of having little. But as an aesthetic concept, it is imbued with the nobility of spirit that comes from practicing a certain austerity. *Wabi* means to transform material insufficiency so that one discovers in it a world of spiritual freedom not bound by material things.

This particular sensitivity first emerged in medieval literary contexts such as *Hōjōki* (The Tale of My Hut) by the recluse aesthete Kamo no Chōmei (1155–1216), who relates his renouncing of urban life for one of spiritual solitude and contemplation of nature, or in the well-known verse by Fujiwara Sadaie (1162–1241):

Miwataseba	In the Autumn dusk
Hanazu mo momiji mo	Looking about
Nakarikeri	Neither flowers
Ura no tomaya no	Nor scarlet leaves,
Aki no yūgo	A bayside hovel

In a complete antithesis of the rich harvest and bright colors normally associated with the fall season, the monotone image here instead is one of a still, lonely emptiness that more than hints at the darkness and cold of the coming winter. This feeling of *wabi* can evoke the rather melancholic picture of a kind of loneliness endured by one who has been bypassed by life's fortunes. In a more noble sense, however, it idealizes the holding of spiritual values—over social status and material things—and finding an exulted satisfaction in the simplest comforts. In *Zen and Japanese Culture*, Zen master and writer Daisetz T. Suzuki (1870–1966) asserts that this virtue is characteristic of the Japanese mind: "Even in the intellectual life, not richness of ideas, not brilliancy or solemnity in marshalling thoughts and building up a philosophical system is sought; but just to stay quietly content with the mystical contemplation of Nature and to feel at home with the world is more inspiring to us, at least to some of us."[2]

Related to *wabi* is the concept *sabi,* likewise associated with quiet, subdued taste, but also connoting age, imperfection, and patina—the beauty born of use—and a certain spiritual solitude. Both *wabi* and *sabi* are sensitivities that have become identified with the spirit of the tea ceremony, which is essentially the layman's practice of Zen.

In *Zen and the Fine Arts,* philosopher Shin'ichi Hisamatsu (1889–1980) proposes seven aesthetic characteristics of objects that express a Zen sensibility: asymmetry; simplicity; astringency or dryness; naturalness; profundity or reserve; non-attachment; and tranquility.[3] As *wabi* taste is so inherently linked to Zen and revealed in the context of tea, which is the focus of this section, it is instructive to review Hisamatsu's analysis to guide our discernment. Observing that symmetry is boring to the mind and deadens the senses, he promotes irregular compositions, whose informality substantiates a familiar human quality and is therefore more natural and interesting. A superb black Mino tea bowl (Plate 31), unusual in its triangular form, expresses this taste for asymmetry in the context of tea. In simplicity and astringency (*shibui*), the discipline of editing out all that is superfluous lends an appreciation for restraint, minimalism, and the basic excellence of an underlying form, as in the superb iron kettle once owned by Sen no Rikyū (Plate 29). The natural ash glazes of Shigaraki ware, favored by tea masters for use as water jars (Plate 30) and tea bowls (Plate 33), express this appreciation for spontaneous gesture and natural unaffected surfaces.

In the *wabi* ideal, the whole is not revealed at once, but certain qualities are kept hidden in reserve for the viewer to seek out, to discover in its handling or with the hint of a poetic reference. Profundity also suggests a certain darkness—the shadows of a tearoom where early morning or evening light is filtered through bamboo-slatted windows, a calm darkness conducive to contemplation. Negoro lacquer, a type of ware created by Buddhist monks, is characterized by a palimpsest effect of streaking black over red lacquer, suggesting a darkening over time. A magnificent ceremonial wine ewer (Plate 28) expresses this *wabi* ideal where the unknown and unseen holds the essence of Japanese art. A certain gloom is important in most areas of traditional Japanese aesthetics: paradoxically, under too much light the beauty of much Japanese art can be extinguished.

Hisamatsu goes on to praise non-attachment and tranquility, the free spirit of a Zen adept who rejects anything that is formulaic, inflexible, or bound by regulations and who lives instead within the creative spirit of nature. The great haiku poet Bashō counts himself among the legendary Zen masters, and artists Saigyō, Soōgi, Sesshū, and Rikyū who have embraced the spirit of *furyū,* a refined solitude that embraces *wabi*, Zen austerity, as life's ideal.

The difference between the Japanese taste for Artless Simplicity (*soboku*) and Zen Austerity *(wabi)* is defined by context. Both value simplicity, unaffectedness, naturalness. But where one describes utilitarian objects of rural life, a kind of folk art, the other is a highly cultivated approach to objects used in the tea ceremony and in the daily life of an aesthete. *Wabi* objects are less made than chosen, and it is in their arrangement as utensils in a tearoom that their aesthetic is fully realized.

1. Daisetz T. Suzuki, *Zen and Japanese Culture* (Princeton, NJ: Princeton University Press, 1970), p. 23.

2. Ibid., p. 23.

3. Shin'ichi Hisamatsu, *Zen and the Fine Arts*. Translated by Gishin Tokiwa (Tokyo and New York: Kodansha International, 1971). Originally published in Japanese in 1957.

PLATE 28
Sake Vessel
Muromachi period, 15th–16th century
Negoro ware; red lacquer
30.5 x 16.6 cm
Brooklyn Museum of Art, Gift of Robert B. Woodward, by exchange and the Oriental Art Acquisitions Fund (74.4)

Negoro lacquer wares are named after the Negoro temple complex located in Wakayama Prefecture (south of present-day Osaka) that served as headquarters for a faction of the Shingon sect of Buddhism. Originally Negoro lacquer was a type of functional, undecorated ware that was made for everyday and ritual use by the monks at the Negoro temple. Their sturdy forms were generally coated with red lacquer over black, like this fine example. Lacquer-making was identified with this area for some three centuries before the temple was destroyed by Toyotomi Hideyoshi in 1585.

The word Negoro is now generically used to describe many wares with red lacquer applied over black lacquer. With use, the surface layer of red lacquer gradually wears through to expose random areas of black beneath; Negoro wares are highly prized for this effect. Such traces of time and wear came to be appreciated from the late sixteenth century as the essence of *wabi* taste.

Vessels of this shape were originally used to hold ritual offerings of sake on an altar. The wood was turned on a lathe and hollowed about halfway down the bottle. This gave a satisfying stability and weight to this classical form.   [M.D.]

PLATE 29
Kettle, known as *Taya Itome*
Late Muromachi-early Momoyama period, 16th century
Cast iron, bronze lid
17.5 x 13.5 x 29 cm
Peggy and Richard M. Danziger Collection

Iron kettles have been made at Temmyō in Sano City, modern-day Tochigi Prefecture, north of Tokyo, since metal craftsmen, who were probably of Korean descent, moved to the area during the Heian period (974–1185). Temmyō kettles made for tea-ceremony use are usually undecorated, with aesthetic emphasis being more directed toward the basic shape and the surface texture of the iron. Characteristically they show a clearly defined, straight-sided mouth, as in this exceptional example.

The top part of the kettle has a cast design of narrow, parallel, raised bands, which may have

inspired the name that was given to the piece: *Taya Itome* ("continuous thread"). Like most objects that have been collected or adapted for use in the tea ceremony, poetic names were given by the connoisseur-tea master who originally owned the object. In some cases, the artist who made the work named it.

This kettle was owned by Sen no Rikyū, who is recognized for refining the *wabi* ideal in tea—an aesthetic of cultivated simplicity and poverty, of richness veiled in austerity. It later belonged to Baron Masuda Takashi (1848–1938), an eminent collector, connoisseur, and tea master of the early modern period.   [M.D.]

Plate 30
Water Jar
Late Muromachi period, 16th century
Shigaraki ware; stoneware with natural-ash glaze, black lacquer lid
20 x 17.7 cm
Peggy and Richard M. Danziger Collection

Containers of this shape were traditionally used for soaking bast fibers before spinning them to make linen. The rustic quality of such objects was seen as consistent with the aesthetics of *wabi*. Ceramic vessels of similar shape were made for use in the tea ceremony as water jars (*mizusashi*). This example of Shigaraki wares has been sculpted with a spatula, creating an interesting surface; the wide mouth is fitted with a black lacquer lid.   [M.D.]

PLATE 31
Tea Bowl
Momoyama period, 16th–17th century
Mino ware, Black Oribe type; glazed stoneware
8.4 x 17 x 13.8 cm
Private Collection

This unctuous, dense black glaze was achieved by removing the vessel from the kiln at the peak of the firing process to cool it rapidly. Had the piece been left in the kiln to cool slowly, the glaze would have become more brown. The frothy green tea used in the tea ceremony looks particularly attractive against such soft black glazes. Black Oribe ware was an icon of *wabi* taste, and this bowl epitomizes that aesthetic with its quiet, undecorated surface, its asymmetrical shape, and the sculptural ridges left by the potter's fingers when the bowl was made.   [M.D.]

PLATE 32
Tea Bowl
Edo period, 18th century
Red Raku ware; glazed earthenware
5.5 x 13.8 cm
Peggy and Richard M. Danziger Collection

During the 1570s, the Raku kiln was established by the potter Chōjirō (1516–1592) in Kyoto under the direction of the tea master Sen no Rikyū for the purpose of making tea ceremony wares. The kiln, which continued under the Raku family to the present day, is identified with making tea bowls (chawan). These bowls are usually formed by hand and squeezed into shape by and smoothed off with a wooden spatula, rather than thrown on a potter's wheel.

Soft, local earthenware clay is used to make the body, which is then covered with a glaze that fuses at a low temperature. A Raku-ware tea bowl is insulated by its thick walls and can be handled comfortably even when containing hot tea.

This bowl's shallow shape allows the tea to cool more rapidly and is therefore more appropriate for summer tea ceremonies. The thin glaze has worn off around the rim of the bowl, exposing the clay body, an effect known in Japanese as mushi-kui (insect-nibbled).   [M.D.]

PLATE 33
Tea Bowl
Momoyama period, early 17th century
Shigaraki ware; stoneware with natural-ash glaze
9.7 x 8.3 cm
Peggy and Richard M. Danziger Collection

With their quiet, rustic shapes and pleasing color variations, Shigaraki pieces were among the first Japanese wares to be adopted for use in wabi tea. An intellectual play on rustic qualities can be seen in the square, spatula-formed foot and the "just right" siting of the patch of natural ash glaze—hinting that a tea master had a hand in the design. Although it is impossible to control exactly what happens in a wood-burning kiln, this tea bowl (chawan) may have been placed where it would stand the best chance of having the ash melt into the attractive scenery seen here, because the wabi aesthetic condoned such contrived "simplicity."   [M.D.]

PLATE 34
Charcoal Basket
Meiji period, late 19th–early 20th century
Woven bamboo, cane
12 x 25 cm
Peggy and Richard M. Danziger Collection

Baskets of this type held the charcoal used for heating water in a tea ceremony; the tools also included metal chopsticks for handling the charcoal, a metal spoon for arranging the ash, and a small brush made of feathers to sweep the ash. Bamboo develops a beautiful, soft patina with age and use, a quality identified with wabi, and so this material is appreciated in objects made for the tea ceremony. Baskets used for containing charcoal (sumitori) were usually lined with lacquered paper to contain any loose dust.   [M.D.]

PLATE 35
Vase
Muromachi period, 16th century
Bronze
24.8 x 8.5 x 5.2 cm
Peggy and Richard M. Danziger Collection

This vase was made by the lost-wax method of bronze casting. Its mouth is in the outline of a Chinese bellflower, one of the seven classic flowers of autumn. It would have been used for a simple, natural arrangement of one or two wildflowers to be placed in the display alcove (tokonoma) of a tearoom. The material, severe shape, and lack of any surface decoration express the wabi ideal of austerity.   [M.D.]

PLATE 36
Hanging Flower Basket
Hayakawa Shōkosai II (1840–1905)
Meiji Period
Woven rattan, wood
24.1 x 17.1 x 8.9 cm
Lloyd and Margit Cotsen Collection

The craft of basketry has reached its apotheosis in Japan, pushed by inexhaustible inventiveness in the use of bamboo. The many varieties of this plant are found there are widely valued for resilience and toughness. The proportions and aesthetic of this rustic hanging container are appropriate for a small tea room where it would complement the simple wild grasses of a summer arrangement.   [M.D.]

PLATE 37
Flower Basket
Early Showa period, dated 1926
Woven bamboo
27.9 x 38.1 cm
Peggy and Richard M. Danziger Collection

This is one of seven copies of a famous basket whose provenance can be traced to Sen no Rikyū, who adapted a basket originally designed to hold fresh-caught fish as a flower container. The original was acquired by the Meiji industrialist, tea master, and art collector, Baron Masuda Takashi. After it passed through the hands of successive connoisseurs, Masuda commissioned seven copies, which he gave as gifts to his collector friends.   [M.D.]

PLATE 38
Mukōzuke Dish
Momoyama period, early 17th century
Mino ware, Oribe type; glazed stoneware with iron slip,
underglaze iron painting, and copper glaze
9.5 x 8.4 cm
Brooklyn Museum of Art, Gift of Robert B. Woodward
(03.87)

Small dishes used for serving delicacies accompanying a tea ceremony were usually made in sets of
five, with more-or-less similar shape and decoration.
The presentation of food has been elevated to a high
art in Japan, reaching an apotheosis in *kaiseki,* the
meal associated with the tea ceremony. Pieces used
for this meal, like this *mukōzuke,* complement the
food, with particular attention paid to color, texture,
and appropriate seasonal nuances. The indented
outline of this vessel suggests the shape of a flower;
it is decorated with a simple V-shaped design in
underglaze iron oxide and a glassy green glaze,
which has dribbled down the sides.   [M.D.]

PLATE 39
Set of *Mukōzuke* Dishes
Edo period, late 18th–early 19th century
Kyoto ware, attributed to Omuro kiln; glazed stoneware,
iron-oxide design
4.5 x 11 x 7 cm
Peggy and Richard M. Danziger Collection

These small bowls, used for serving individual
delicacies in the elaborate *kaiseki* meal that
inaugurated more formal tea ceremonies, remain
from what was probably an original set of five. The
soft-fired Kyoto-type pottery shows faint bluish iron
oxide markings under a translucent glaze with a fine
crackle. Before firing, the soft clay was carefully
squeezed to make a shape similar to that of straw
hats worn during summer festivals. Their simple,
unadorned surface and asymmetrical form would
make these vessels a natural choice for use in *wabi*
tea.   [M.D.]

PLATE 40
Two-tiered Food Box
Momoyama period, 17th century
Mino ware, Shino type; glazed stoneware, iron-oxide
design
14 x 15 x 15 cm
Victor and Takako Hauge Collection

Shino wares, made at the Mino complex of kilns in
Gifu Prefecture since the late sixteenth century, are
famous for sugary, feldspathic glazes. At the
beginning of the seventeenth century, a new type of
climbing kiln was introduced that was capable of
being fired to higher temperatures than had
previously been achieved. As a result, the milky
glaze became thinner and clearer, allowing any
underglaze decoration to be clearly seen. This set of

stacking food containers is typical of these later
Shino wares; this type was used at outdoor tea
ceremonies or for less formal meals. The design,
sketched in underglaze iron-oxide, of a few reeds and
a couple of fish nets hanging up to dry evokes the
end of a late summer day when dusk is gathering
and all work has ceased. The poetic connotation
hints at the changing season and conjures the
contemplative and restrained mood associated with
wabi sensitivities.   [M.D.]

PLATE 41
Plate
Momoyama period, late 16th–early 17th century
Mino ware, Gray Shino type; glazed stoneware, iron slip,
incised design
22.4 x 19.6 cm
Peggy and Richard M. Danziger Collection

The geometric border on this plate encloses a
design of plants with pointed leaves radiating from
spaced nodes that look like thoroughwort. To achieve
this effect, the dish was first covered with an iron-
bearing slip and the design incised through the slip
to the white clay with a sharpened piece of bamboo
or a metal tool before glazing and firing. Four marks
reveal where balls of clay were placed to separate
this from other dishes stacked for firing in the kiln.

Such large dishes, used to serve food—particularly
traditional sweets and cakes—to the assembled
guests at a tea ceremony, were carefully chosen to
complement the colors and textures of the food
served and were in harmony with the occasion and
season. As food was removed with chopsticks by
each guest, revealing more of the design, the
aesthetic enjoyment of the piece was completed.
[M.D.]

PLATE 42
Kasuga Tray
Kamakura–early Muromachi period, 14th century
Negoro ware; red and black lacquer with mother-of-pearl
inlay
37.8 x 28.2 x 4 cm
Peggy and Richard M. Danziger Collection

The craftsmen working at the Negoro temple
complex made lacquer wares not only for local use
but also for more distant customers within Japan. An
inscription on the box accompanying this tray
indicates that it was owned by the Kasuga Shrine at
the Tōdai-ji temple in Nara. This tray is a true
example of beauty born of use: the red surface has
worn through to the black layer underneath, forming
an abstract pattern. The underside of the tray is
black lacquer with four mother-of-pearl inlays that
depict long-tailed birds and flora; this rare decorative
element suggests that this piece was commissioned
for special use.   [M.D.]

PLATE 43
Sake Bottle

Momoyama period, late 16th century
Mino ware, Oribe type; stoneware, iron-oxide design on slip-covered body, copper green glaze
17.8 x 9.5 cm
Asia Society, The Mr. and Mrs. John D. Rockefeller 3rd Collection (1979.227)

The image of eulalia grass *(susuki)* suggests the season when new sake will become available for drinking and also evokes autumn and the coming of winter. The feeling is a poignant reminder of the transience of life that resonates with Buddhist teaching and fits with the "beauty in sadness" aesthetic ideals of *wabi* taste.

A sake bottle such as this would have been appropriate for use in a tea ceremony meal, which always contains references to the season. Oribe wares are products of the Mino kilns in the Gifu Prefecture, which specialized in tea-ceremony utensils, and many characteristically show decoration in underglaze iron and a green glaze.   [M.D.]

PLATE 44
Sake Cup

Momoyama period, early 17th century
Hagi ware; stoneware with white slip brushed on under clear glaze
4.3 x 6.2 cm
Peggy and Richard M. Danziger Collection

The kilns located around the city of Hagi, in present-day Yamaguchi Prefecture on the Japan Sea, were established by immigrant Korean potters at the beginning of the seventeenth century. Hagi wares consist mostly of small cups, bowls, and dishes commissioned for the tea ceremony. These vessels are undecorated so that the wonderful effect of the pink-orange body showing through a white slip under a transparent glaze is revealed.

This sake cup shows the influence of earlier Korean brushed-slip wares in the rough wipe of white glaze around the irregular shape. Tiny crystals of quartz in the clay have burst during firing to create an interesting "landscape" with small pits and fissures. [M.D.]

PLATE 28
Sake Vessel
Muromachi period, 15th–16th century
Brooklyn Museum of Art

PLATE 29
Kettle, known as *Taya Itome*
Late Muromachi-early Momoyama period, 16th century
Peggy and Richard M. Danziger Collection

PLATE 30
Water Jar
Late Muromachi period, 16th century
Peggy and Richard M. Danziger Collection

PLATE 31
Tea Bowl
Momoyama period, 16th–17th century
Private Collection

PLATE 32
Tea Bowl
Edo period, 18th century
Peggy and Richard M. Danziger Collection

PLATE 33
Tea Bowl
Momoyama period, early 17th century
Peggy and Richard M. Danziger Collection

PLATE 34
Charcoal Basket
Meiji period, late 19th–early 20th century
Peggy and Richard M. Danziger Collection

PLATE 35
Vase
Muromachi period, 16th century
Peggy and Richard M. Danziger Collection

PLATE 36
Hanging Flower Basket
Meiji period, 19th century
Lloyd and Margit Cotsen Collection

PLATE 37
Flower Basket
Early Showa period, dated 1927
Peggy and Richard M. Danziger Collection

PLATE 38
Mukōzuke Dish
Momoyama period, early 17th century
Brooklyn Museum of Art

PLATE 39
Set of _Mukōzuke_ Dishes
Edo period, late 18th–early 19th century
Peggy and Richard M. Danziger Collection

PLATE 40
Two-tiered Food Box
Momoyama period, 17th century
Victor and Takako Hauge Collection

PLATE 41
Plate
Momoyama period, late 16th–early 17th century
Peggy and Richard M. Danziger Collection

PLATE 42
Kasuga Tray
Kamakura-early Muromachi period, 14th century
Peggy and Richard M. Danziger Collection

PLATE 43
Sake Bottle
Momoyama period, late 16th century
Asia Society, The Mr. and Mrs. John D. Rockefeller 3rd Collection

PLATE 44
Sake Cup
Momoyama period, early 17th century
Peggy and Richard M. Danziger Collection

GORGEOUS SPLENDOR

 *Karei*

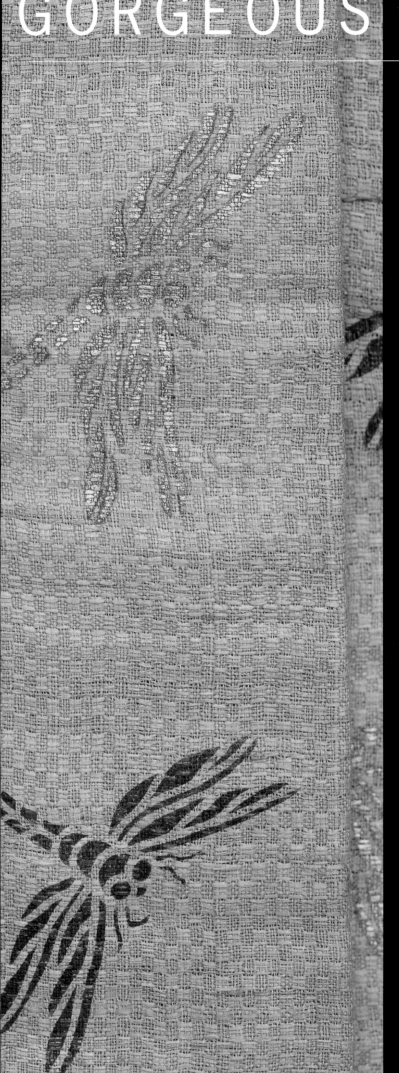

Gorgeous Splendor

Karei

*And surely you have seen, in the darkness of the innermost rooms of these huge buildings,
to which sunlight never penetrates, how the gold leaf of a sliding door or screen will pick up
a distant glimmer from the garden, then suddenly send forth an ethereal glow, a faint golden
light cast into the enveloping darkness, like the glow upon the horizon at sunset.*

Tanizaki Jun'ichirō, In Praise of Shadows (1934) [1]

THE TASTE FOR GORGEOUS SPLENDOR in Japanese culture was largely expressed by members of the imperial family and its court, the shogun and regional daimyo, and to lesser nobles and upper ranks of the samurai class. With origins in the cultural tastes of the Ashikaga shogunate (1338–1573), *karei* aesthetics flowered in the Momoyama (1573–1615) and Edo periods (1615–1868). Unlike Artless Simplicity (*soboku*) or Zen Austerity (*wabi*), which are based on concepts of beauty in poverty, *karei* taste is associated with an unabashed display of wealth.

Until the peaceful unification of the country under the Tokugawa shogunate in 1615, warlords had risen and fallen with the complex political and military upheavals of the preceding centuries. Some were aristocrats with ancient bloodlines (*shugo*) who had absorbed the literary and artistic tastes of the imperial court, and all but a few daimyo—and those exceptions lived in remote fiefs—espoused a balance of military virtues (*bu*) and civilian arts (*bun*) as ideals for the warrior-elite. Those daimyo who had risen to power without hereditary connections needed to learn new skills such as writing and bureaucratic organization, to govern effectively. These they studied in the households of hereditary nobles or at leading Buddhist temples and monasteries. By such associations military men also learned finer cultural tastes, and, in taking on aristocratic manners, turned to such courtly interests as the Noh drama, tea ceremony, painting, calligraphy, and poetry.

Throughout the Edo period, with the country more or less at peace under the control of the Tokugawa shoguns and their regional daimyo, military virtues underscored power but were rarely put to practice. With more time free for cultural pursuits and luxurious living, daimyo of all levels developed tastes for Gorgeous Splendor. The daimyo were obliged by edict of the shogun to maintain suitable residences in the capital of Edo (present-day Tokyo), in addition to their own regional castles. Further, they were required to reside in Edo on a regular alternating basis, during which the protocol of their duties at the shogun's court required the highest standards of appearance. An enormous service industry developed to sustain this magnificence, and with it appeared a new breed of merchants and talented artisans.

The personal effects of a daimyo were divided into those required for his official position (*omote-dōgu*), and those for his private use (*oku-dōgu*). Weapons and accoutrements needed for battle and official pageantry, for the corps of samurai retainers and their horses, as well as the paraphernalia of hunting and falconry—sports of a suitably military nature—fell into the former category. In this section, superb examples of arms and armor, including fine swords and their elaborate mountings, express the essence of Gorgeous Splendor: technical virtuosity; rich materials including gold, precious inlay, and lacquer; and highly decorated surfaces that express both the refinement and spectacle of the ruling military taste (Plates 49–53). Campaign coats (*jimbaori*), designed to be worn over suits of armor and for military parades, were also a vehicle for the display of Gorgeous Splendor (Plates 45–48).

In their castles and palaces the military class sumptuously decorated reception rooms to be used for official purposes and entertaining guests. *Karei* taste valued the use of gold (and to a lesser extent, silver) in the decoration of architecture and objects. Gold particularly was prized for its quality of reflecting light, however dim the source—thereby brightening the gloom of dark interiors where the only light after sunset came from oil lamps and candles. The Japanese were skilled at making gold leaf used to decorate screen paintings and sliding doors, either sprinkled in flakes or dust onto a surface prepared with adhesive, or applied in cut-out shapes. Gold, in the form of dust or flakes, was often used in a variety of lacquer-making techniques, for example, in a fine wash basin decorated in Kodai-ji *maki-e* (Plate 54) . Fine porcelains (Plate 55) were essential elements of the daimyo household, as were tea rooms in a range of styles. The aesthetic contrast between the rich appointments of the main reception rooms and the "humble" utensils used in tea ceremonies underscored that the latter often had greater value and prestige.

The private furnishings and ornaments of the daimyo household included clothing and the many accessories of personal grooming. Women of a daimyo household enjoyed exquisitely made robes, mirror stands, cosmetic boxes, and accessories (Plates 56–58), and numerous items for the presentation of food (Plates 60, 64), writing letters (Plate 59), music-making and other pastimes of cultivated living. The quality of the materials used in making objects in *karei* taste was designed to impress, but skill and artistry were likewise factors in calculating their value. The products of samurai discipline combined with aristocratic taste—*bu* and *bun*—met peerless standards.

The historical context of *karei* taste, which arose with the concentrated wealth of a feudal society, assured its doom. By the mid-Edo period, wealthy merchants assumed aspects of *karei* taste and patronized some of its finest crafts, such as lacquer and textiles, during the decline of the military elite in the eighteenth and nineteenth centuries. Regardless of who ultimately came to use the objects gathered here, they offer a glimpse of the unsurpassed elegance of Japan's courtly world of Gorgeous Splendor.

1. Tanizaki Jun'ichirō, *In Praise of Shadows*. Translated by Thomas J. Harper and Edward Seidensticker (London: Jonathan Cape, 1991), p. 22.

PLATE 45
Campaign Coat
Edo period, early 19th century
Wool and metallic thread appliqué on wool, lining of silk
and metallic thread lampas
97.8 x 74 cm
John C. Weber Collection

Campaign coats (*jimbaori*) worn from the sixteenth century onward by high-ranking warriors—over armor if they were destined for battle—were often made of imported wool cloth, called *rasha,* that had been treated and shrunk, giving it a felt-like finish. Its warmth, durability, and impermeability were appreciated, and it was highly valued for its exotic, European origin. In the peaceful years of the Tokugawa reign, a *jimbaori* was worn for formal ceremonial occasions as a symbol of status and power.

This coat is made of black wool and lined with silk. The front lapels are turned out and held with silver buttons and silk knotted cords; the shoulder epaulets are silk with silk cords. The torn fan design is an appliqué in white of the same kind of wool cloth as the black background, and the fan's ribs are embroidered in gold thread. In this stunning design, the opened fan is asymmetrically placed to the left of center on the back of the coat; fragments of paper torn from its exposed ribs dangle to the right. This composition expresses the Japanese appreciation of the beauty of imperfection and the transitory nature of things.

The bold designs on *jimbaori* reflected the personal taste of the military elite and were intended to make a strong impression on the battlefield. While the designs on many *jimbaori* derive from European surcoats, the torn fan on this coat is quintessentially Japanese. Because fans were used by military leaders to command soldiers on the battlefield, the tattered fan could suggest defeat. Translated another way, it could also mean "never give up" or "fight to the end," both important principles of the samurai code of honor. [A.V.A.]

PLATES 46 and 47
Campaign Coat
Edo period, mid-19th century
Ink inscription on stencil resist-dyed plain weave silk with
gold leaf
65 x 110 cm
John C. Weber Collection

Sleeveless Campaign Coat
Edo period, mid-19th century
101.2 x 110 cm
Embroidered inscription in silk on silk satin with supplementary weft patterning, lining of woven hemp stenciled in gold leaf and indigo dye
John C. Weber Collection

These two campaign coats, or *jimbaori,* are both decorated with poetry and appear to have been made as a set. On the blue and white silk jacket with a stenciled design of large and small cherry blossoms, the poem is written with brush and ink. On the sleeveless silk jacket with a design of plum blossoms, clouds, and paired undulating lines, the text is embroidered over an ink underdrawing to look as though it had been written with brush and ink. Dragonflies, stenciled on the hemp lining, evoke an ancient name for Japan, *Akizu Shima* (dragonfly island). Both garments represent a tour de force of decorative technique and a taste for luxury.

The poetic inscriptions on both coats are rendered in a mixture of highly cursive Chinese characters, which are read for meaning, and *sogana,* cursive forms of characters that are read phonetically. This deliberately archaic style of calligraphy came back into vogue during the late eighteenth century with the flourishing of the *Kokugaku* (National Learning) movement.

The 31-syllable poem or *waka* on the jacket with cherry blossoms reads:

> *saki-idete hana wa chiru tomo kaguwashiki*
> *nioi wa yoyo ni nokosazarame ya*

> After bursting into bloom, flowers soon scatter, but their sweet-scented
> fragrance will linger generation after generation.

The inscription on the front and back of the sleeveless coat reads:

> *saki-idete*
> *katsu-iro miseyo*

> After bursting into bloom
> show your triumphant colors...

The poetic image of scattering blossoms is a common metaphor for the evanescent life of warriors; here the poem suggests that even though brave men fall in battle their glorious reputations live on "generation after generation," just as the fragrance of flowers can linger after they die. This interpretation is reinforced by the inscription on the sleeveless coat, which recalls a poem likening warriors to the blossoms of wild cherry recorded in chapter 7 of the medieval war tale *Taiheiki*. The original poem—the opening stanza of a *renga* or linked-verse sequence—begins *saki-gakete / katsu-iro miseyo* ("Moving to the front line, show your triumphant colors..."). Both poems superimpose an image of gorgeous blossoms on a scene of warriors in resplendent costume. In the late Edo period, with the country at peace, still we can imagine proud descendants of some noble warrior family commissioning *jimbaori* of this variety for display or parade.

[Nobuko Ochner / John T. Carpenter]

PLATE 48
Samurai Fireman's Coat, Plastron, and Waistband
Edo period, 19th century
Wool appliqué on wool twill, silk and metallic trim, plain-weave silk lining
109.2 x 131.4 cm
John C. Weber Collection

Only firefighters who worked in the service of military lords wore expensive wool coats like this one, which is made of red cochineal-dyed wool. This fabric is called *goro,* a term thought to be derived from the Dutch *grof grain.* This derivation does not necessarily mean that the fabric, which is a blend of sheep's wool with cashmere goat fibers and camel's hair, was made in the Netherlands, but it was imported from Europe by the beginning of the seventeenth century. Because Japan did not produce wool, this fabric had an obviously exotic origin that lent it prestige. Wool was a good choice for a fire-fighting costume because it has self-extinguishing properties that would help protect the wearer from stray sparks.

These *kajibaori,* literally "fire coats," were complex costumes that identified the wearer as a member of the samurai class. The outfit included a plastron placed over the chest and worn under the coat. The decorated part of the waistband was exposed on the back side; it was threaded through holes in the side of the coat and tied over the plastron in front. There is a variation of the Watanabe family crest appliquéd on the back of this coat. [A.V.A.]

PLATE 49
Sword (*tachi* type, slung cutting edge down)
Nagamitsu (active late 13th–early 14th century)
Kamakura period
Tempered steel
Length: 80.3; curvature: 2.95 cm
Museum of Fine Arts, Boston, Gift of Mrs. Charles Goddard Weld (13.281)

The Osafune School was founded by Mitsutada in Osafune, Bizen Province, and produced a long line of famed swordsmiths. From the middle of the

Kamakura period onward, the renowned smiths Mitsutada, Nagamitsu, Kagemitsu, and Kanemitsu succeeded one another as masters of the main line of the Osafune School. Osafune was the most prolific of all schools of the Kotō period of sword making (late tenth through sixteenth century) and prospered until the late Muromachi period. Nagamitsu is believed to have been either the son or pupil of Mitsutada.

The special characteristic of the temper lines of the Osafune School is a regular wavy or zigzag pattern known as *gunome-midare*. Nagamitsu, however, exhibits the trademark style of the Fukuoka Ichimonji School: a tempering pattern of fine iron carbide crystals that give a misty appearance (*nioi*) arranged with a clove-shaped wave pattern known as *choji-midare* that incorporates intermittent *gunome-midare*. This unmistakable feature appears also in Mitsutada's style, though his *choji-midare* are even more exuberant than those of Nagamitsu.

This *tachi*-type sword is intact in its original form. It has a slender body that follows a refined curve with a center which lies closer to the tang (or projecting shank) and ends in a small point. The fine "wood grain" of the steel surface is brushed with *chikei* and vivid *midare-utsuri*. The edge is tempered with a pattern of small *gunome* of *nioi* structure with small *choji* and small *ashi*.

Two styles appear in Nagamitsu's work; the more subdued style can be seen in this blade; the other style has a much wider blade and more exuberant temper line.   [M.O.]

PLATE 50
Sword (*tachi* type, slung cutting edge down) with Mounting
Kanemitsu (active 14th century)
Late Kamakura-early Nambokuchō period, mid-14th century
Tempered steel
Length: 70.5; curvature: 1.86 cm
Museum of Fine Arts, Boston, Charles Goddard Weld Collection (11.5097a,b)

Kanemitsu is traditionally believed to be the son of Kagemitsu. Extant inscribed blades by Kanemitsu bear dates ranging from Genkō (1321–23) to Ōan (1368–74). Given the length of activity and stylistic considerations, it is commonly believed that two generations of swordsmiths used the name Kanemitsu.

The first generation to use the name Kanemitsu is generally believed to be represented by the style of blades inscribed with a Kamakura period (1185–1333) or early Nambokuchō era (1333–1392) date. The tempering of these blades exhibits Kagemitsu-style: a regular sawtooth pattern (*kataochi-gunome*) combined with a pattern of clove-shaped waves (*gunome-choji midare*). The shape of these *tachi*-type swords is commonly seen in works of the late Kamakura period (1185–1333): the blades are of average width and have a medium point. After the Kanno era (1350–1351) and becoming more numerous around the Embun era (1356–1360), Kanemistu blades are tempered with wide undulating waves. These *tachi* are wider and have a large point, and large *tachi*, over ninety centimeters in length, begin to appear. These later blades represent the style of the so-called second generation of Embun Kanemitsu.

For Kanemitsu, this sword is quite narrow and has a small point. The tempered edge has a bright, clear line between the forged and tempered areas (*nioi-guchi*); the tempered pattern variation (*kataochi-gunome*) contains a sharp clove-like pattern (*choji*); and small, bright lines (*ashi*) extend into the tempering. In addition to these tempering patterns, abundant small crystals (*nie*) appear.

Although this blade is not inscribed with a date, from the style, and especially from the apparent Kagemitsu influence seen in the characteristic *kataochi-gunome*, it can be ascertained as being an early work by Kanemitsu. The accompanying thread-wrapped *tachi* mounting (*itomaki-tachi-goshirae*) dates to no later than the seventeenth century and is of splendid workmanship.   [M.O.]

PLATE 51
Guardless Sword Mounting with Lacquer Sheath
Momoyama period, late 16th–early 17th century
Gold and black lacquer over wood, rayskin, *shakudō*, copper, silk
Length: 54.9; curvature: 1.9 cm
Private Collection

The term *koshigatana goshira-e* refers in general to short sword mountings; when the mounting includes a sword guard (*tsuba*) it is called *chiisagatana goshira-e;* when guardless it is called *aikuchi goshira-e.* Guardless sword mountings were made and used extensively during the Muromachi (1392–1573) and Momoyama periods (1573–1615). However, only a few have survived.

This magnificent composition depicts a chrysanthemum floating upon the whirling surface of a flowing river. The scabbard (*saya*) design is a fine example of the elaborate Kodai-ji *maki-e* lacquer technique that is here composed of two elements: flat gold *maki-e* (*kinhira maki-e*) and *nashiji*, a method of sprinkling gold powder on a black lacquer ground.

The ornamental elements, other than the hilt ornaments (*menuki*), are decorated with heraldic crests (*mon*) in the form of flowers of the paulownia tree. The paulownia crest still retains some gold, which recalls the splendorous beauty of the magnificent age of its creation. The paulownia crest was first used by the imperial family, and later by the Ashikaga shoguns who ruled during the Muromachi period. The powerful samurai warriors who unified Japan after centuries of civil war, Oda Nobunaga (1534–1582) and Toyotomi Hideyoshi (1536–1598), both used this crest.

The use of the Kodai-ji *maki-e* technique and the presence of the paulownia crests indicate that the owner of this sword mounting must have been a relative of Toyotomi Hideyoshi, who favored richly decorative Kodai-ji lacquers, or possibly Hideyoshi himself. [M.O.]

PLATE 52
Sword Guard
Arichika (1661–1742)
Mid-Edo period, 18th century
Copper (*suaka*), gold, *shibuichi*, *shakudō*
7.4 x 7.4 cm
Museum of Fine Arts, Boston, Special Chinese and Japanese Fund (13.2368)

Watanabe Arichika was born in Shonai, Uzen Province (Yamagata Prefecture) in 1661. He first entered the workshop of Satō Yoshihisa (also read "Chinkyū") and afterward went to Edo (present-day Tokyo), where he was influenced by Yasuchika, the famous maker of sword furniture and fellow native of Yamagata Prefecture.

Arichika made many sword guards (*tsuba*) using copper (*suaka*), iron *tetsu*, and a copper alloy mixed with gold that produces a jet-black color (*shakudō*). Many excellent examples made with *suaka* copper still remain.

This sword guard displays wisteria petals that are executed in a flat-ground relief (*hira-zōgan*). The wisteria flowers, with their flat gold inlay, occupy the entire surface of the *tsuba*, and the space between the flowers is pierced to produce a positive silhouette. Ringed with a rim made of a copper and silver alloy (*shibuichi*), this very colorful and stylish *tsuba* is a masterpiece by Arichika.   [M.O.]

PLATE 53
Suit of Armor (*Gusoku* type)
Edo period, 18th century
Lacquered iron, *shakudō*, mail, silk
148.8 x 49.5 cm
Private Collection

The basic style of Japanese armor was established before the mid-tenth century. The so-called official armor (*yoroi*), composed of a cuirass with four-sided skirts (*kusazuri*), was generally worn by warriors on horseback and used from the mid-tenth to fourteenth centuries. The *domaru* and *haramaki* types, worn from the fourteenth to the sixteenth centuries, and *gusoku* type, worn from the sixteenth to nineteenth centuries, are cuirass with seven to nine-sided skirts and were generally worn by warriors who fought on foot.

The style of Japanese armor changed historically as methods of warfare evolved. From the Ōnin War (1467–1477) until the establishment of the Tokugawa shogunate in 1615, Japan was beset by a protracted state of civil war. The infantry troops waged their battles primarily by wielding spears (*yari*), halberds (*nagimata*), and bows. Following the introduction of the matchlock gun from Portugal in 1543, the use of firearms along with spears required a structural change in Japanese armor.

The traditional *yoroi*, *domaru*, and *haramaki* types of armor, which were composed of scales (*kozane*), were clearly not strong enough to protect against spears and bullets. The cuirass thus developed to include layers of several thin iron boards or plates to which seven or eight pieces of sided-skirts (*kusazuri*) were attached. These additions greatly improved the infantry samurai's fighting capacities. Further, shoulder guards (*sode*), helmets (*kabuto*), gauntlets (*kote*), masks (*hoate*), greaves (*suneate*) and thigh guards (*haidate*) were added for protection. A complete set of such armor is called *tosei gusoku*.

This *gusoku*-type armor is a unique example of *gindami-nuri*, an allover paint application of silver powder mixed with Japanese lacquer. The quietly elegant style of this set reflects the taste of its original owner, who must have been a high-ranking samurai and member of the nobility. The comma-shape crest (*mitsudomoe mon*) on this armor is that of the Okabe family, who was the feudal lord of Kishiwada (present-day Kishiwada City in Osaka Prefecture).   [M.O.]

PLATE 54
Wash Basin
Momoyama period, early 17th century
Gold and black lacquer, metal fittings
20.3 x 43.7 cm
John C. Weber Collection

This wash basin is lavishly decorated with a design of paulownia trees that wrap around the exterior in sprinkled gold (*maki-e*) on black lacquer in the Kodai-ji temple style favored by the ruling elite. A ewer with a similar design motif, which would have been stored in the basin when not in use, most likely completed the set. Such luxurious objects were made by the most skilled craftsmen of the finest materials; they displayed the owner's power, wealth, and privilege. The metal fittings have a butterfly crest, indicating that this basin was commissioned by the Ikeda family.   [M.D.]

PLATE 55
Jar
Edo period, 18th century
Arita ware; porcelain painted with underglaze cobalt-blue and enamels
30.5 x 24.1 cm
Philadelphia Museum of Art, Taylor Fund (1955-10-1)

The design of this large jar is quite different from the typical style of Arita porcelain wares of this period, which were influenced by Chinese models and have surfaces often covered with painted detail. The craftsman who enameled this jar in a very painterly style has respected the shape of the vessel and used blank white space to masterly effect as a balance to the design. The decoration shows the influence of Rinpa school paintings, with a bamboo trellis covered with a clematis vine and hanging tendrils that appear almost calligraphic. The combination of peerless quality with a refined artistic scheme is characteristic of aristocratic *karei* taste during the Edo period.   [M.D.]

PLATE 56
Woman's *Kosode* Robe
Edo period, late 17th century
Stencil-dyed and embroidered figured satin silk
158.7 x 119.4 cm
Philadelphia Museum of Art, Gift of Mr. and Mrs. Rodolphe Meyer de Schaensee (1951-42-1)

This *kosode* is an excellent example of a type that was fashionable among the wives of wealthy merchants in the Genroku era (1688–1704). The composition wraps asymmetrically around the body: the design originates at the bottom right of the garment back, moves upward along the side seam, and spreads across the back along the shoulders. Because the left front is visible when the garment is closed, that panel is more elaborately decorated.

The wealthy merchants of the Genroku era demanded a distinctive and new style of *kosode* to differentiate themselves from the privileged elite. They could both enjoy their wealth and reaffirm their cultural values by their tastes in dress. While the elite wore robes decorated with simple, conventionalized motifs, merchants delighted in wearing richly decorated *kosode* with bold designs.

This *kosode* is made of a lustrous figured satin woven with a key fret, chrysanthemum, and orchid pattern. The realistic imagery, borrowed from nature— bamboo hedges, a blooming mandarin orange tree— is typical of Genroku-style designs. The main outline of this design was delicately painted with brush and ink. The motif was stenciled with a technique that imitates tie-dye; after the stenciling, silk thread and silver and gold couched embroidery was applied. [A.V.A.]

PLATE 57
Woman's *Kosode* Robe
Edo period, early 19th century
Embroidered figured satin silk
172.7 x 117.5 cm
John C. Weber Collection

Kosode (literally "small sleeve," a reference to the small opening of the sleeve not to its length) is a full-length garment made prior to the Meiji period that was a predecessor of the modern kimono. A luxurious garment like this example would have been worn by a woman of the samurai class. It is probably a type of *kosode,* called *uchikake,* that was worn as an overrobe. In the later Edo period the garments of samurai women were more likely to be embroidered; those worn by the prosperous townswomen tended to be decorated primarily with dye techniques.

This woman's *kosode* is made of lustrous white silk with a bamboo pattern woven in the figured satin. It is embroidered over its entire surface with motifs of wild ginger and lozenge-shaped crests; the repeated image of oxcart wheels (*genji-guruma*) is, as the Japanese term reveals, an allusion to the classic novel, the *Tale of Genji*. The lining of orange-dyed silk is also used for the padded hem, reflecting late Edo-period style.   [A.V.A.]

PLATE 58
Woman's *Kosode* Robe
Edo period, early 19th century
Resist-dyed and embroidered silk crepe
149.9 x 121.9 cm
Philadelphia Museum of Art, The S. S. White III and Vera
White Collection (1967-30-321)

In the second half of the eighteenth century, a new fashion trend developed: designs done with fewer colors on a dark ground and limited to the lower half of the garment replaced overall patterns with large colorful motifs. This shift in taste mirrored the move of Japan's cultural center from Kyoto-Osaka to Edo (Tokyo), and contemporary trends in Edo soon became the dominant national style.

The design used to decorate this robe is rendered with a technique that evolved during the era of Edo's cultural ascendancy. In the *shiroage nui-iri* technique (literally "finished in white with embroidery"), the design is drawn with rice paste, which remains white when the ground is dyed. The motifs, in this case, autumn flowers and grasses and eight different cricket cages, are then developed with embroidery. A graduated shading technique was used to feather white areas that are meant to suggest early evening mist among the plants. The theme of cricket cages set out among autumn flowers and grasses evokes chapter 28 of the early eleventh-century Japanese epic novel, the *Tale of Genji*, in which several young girls search in a dewy garden for crickets.

The family crest identified as "three wrapped fans" is repeated five times on this garment, which indicates that it would have been worn only on formal occasions. The hem is slightly padded, and the garment is lined with a red silk in late Edo-period style. [A.V.A.]

PLATE 59
Writing Box and Matching Table
Yukio Setsuyū (d. 1926)
Meiji period, late 19th–early 20th century
Gold lacquer with gold and silver inlay, silver fittings
Box: 24.8 x 22.9 x 5.1 cm
Table: 61 x 36.8 x 12.4 cm
The Florence and Herbert Irving Collection

Although this writing ensemble was made some time after the fall of the Tokugawa shogunate, a wealthy aristocracy survived during the Meiji period that maintained the luxurious *karei* style and customs. A certain conservatism can be seen in the work of such major craftsmen as Yukio Setsuyū, who defied the artistic confusion that flooded Japanese traditions after Western ideas were introduced.

This writing table (*bundai*) shows an ancient pine tree on the shore, rendered in fine gold *maki-e* lacquer and lighted by a full moon, inlaid in silver. The writing box displays a stand of pine trees on the cover; and

cranes soar above a reed-lined inlet. The theme of cranes continues on the handles of the writing implements. A silver water-dropper takes the shape of two sailing boats.

Literary themes from the *Kokinshu*, an early imperial anthology of poetry, and the classic Noh play *Takasago* are evoked by the pine trees, which, like cranes, are auspicious symbols of longevity and conjugal fidelity. This symbolism suggests that this writing set was given as a wedding present. [M.D.]

PLATE 60
Pair of Sake Bottles
Momoyama period, late 16th century
Gold on black lacquer
Height: 20.3 cm
Peggy and Richard M. Danziger Collection

With the country at peace under the ruling Tokugawa shogunate, Japan enjoyed economic prosperity and the arts flourished. Large snowflakes falling on bamboo make a rich and spectacular design in lacquer on these sake bottles. These splendid bottles were probably part of a picnic set (*jubako*) with food containers and carrying case decorated with the same snow-on-bamboo motif, an image evocative of spring, which commenced on New Year's Day according to the traditional East Asian calendar. [M.D.]

PLATE 61
Covered Dish
Ogata Kenzan (1663–1743)
Edo period, early 18th century
Kenzan ware; glazed stoneware with slip design, underglaze iron-oxide, cobalt-blue and copper glaze
Signed: *Kenzan*
8.5 x 14.4 cm
Philadelphia Museum of Art, Purchased with John T. Morris Fund (1980-45-1 a,b)

Along with his brother Ogata Kōrin, Kenzan experimented with various artistic pursuits and was adept at both painting and calligraphy. But he is most famous for ceramics. His works, many of which carry his signature on the base, can be divided roughly into two groups; plain, transparent-glazed wares with dark underglaze paintings that often show Zen subjects inspired by his own practice of the discipline; and bold, brightly colored enameled pieces such as this.

In the artistic milieu of Kyoto in his time, Kenzan successfully trod the precarious path of balancing the use of bright colors with good taste; with a sure eye he succeeded in adapting two-dimensional painting designs to the forms of three-dimensional objects. This covered box would have been used for cakes traditionally offered before a tea ceremony. The motif of the moon and grasses evokes early autumn, a seasonal transition celebrated in many aspects of Japanese art and culture. [M.D.]

PLATE 62
Set of *Mukōzuke* Dishes
Momoyama period, late 16th–early 17th century
Mino ware, Yellow Seto type; glazed stoneware, incised
design, touches of iron-oxide and copper green glaze
Each approximately 6 x 8.4 cm
Peggy and Richard M. Danziger Collection

The Mino kilns, established by Seto potters who had
fled hostilities during the late sixteenth century,
quickly earned a reputation for producing high-quality
utensils for tea ceremony use. Ki-Seto (Yellow Seto)
wares like these dishes are identified by an attractive, straw-colored glaze. Touches of copper and
iron add interesting darker patches to this design,
and the color is also richer where the glaze has slid
down the surface and collected just above the base.
Mino ware was also highly prized for such simple,
incised decoration on clay as these grasses,
executed with a few strokes of a tool.   [M.D.]

PLATE 63
Tea Bowl
Momoyama period, early 17th century
Mino ware, Black Oribe type; glazed stoneware, iron-oxide
design
7.2 x 14 cm
Peggy and Richard M. Danziger Collection

At the end of the sixteenth century, some eight kilns
in the Mino area made the distinctive wares known
as Oribe, named for Furuta Oribe (1544–1615)—a
samurai and arbiter of tea taste—who is reputed to
have been a patron and adviser of the kilns. Oribe
wares are noted for their expressive designs and
were largely commissioned for use in the tea
ceremony and its accompanying *kaiseki* meal.
Although Furuta Oribe was a pupil of Sen no Rikyū—
the exponent of *wabi* aesthetics in tea—his taste in
ceramic designs exhibits a more expressive and
exuberant style favored by cultivated samurai, like
himself, and wealthy merchants. For this reason, it
exemplifies the possibilities for *karei* taste in the tea
ceremony. This tea bowl has in an irregular form and
is boldly decorated with geometric roundels painted
in iron-oxide. [M.D.]

PLATE 64
Three-tiered Food Box
Edo period, 17th century
Gold, silver and black lacquer with mother-of-pearl inlay
19.2 x 13.5 x 15 cm
Peggy and Richard M. Danziger Collection

Food containers like this *jubako,* which has three tiers,
made ideal picnic sets. Early autumn is evoked by
susuki grasses rendered in gold *maki-e;* both a full
moon and a three-day moon have been ingeniously
depicted by using gold and silver lacquer, and the
grasses have been depicted wtih inlaid mother-of-pearl
on a black background to suggest the effect of
moonlight. [M.D.]

PLATE 45
Campaign Coat
Edo period, early 19th century
John C. Weber Collection

PLATE 46
Campaign Coat
Edo period, mid-19th century
John C. Weber Collection

PLATE 47
Sleeveless Campaign Coat
Edo period, mid-19th century
John C. Weber Collection

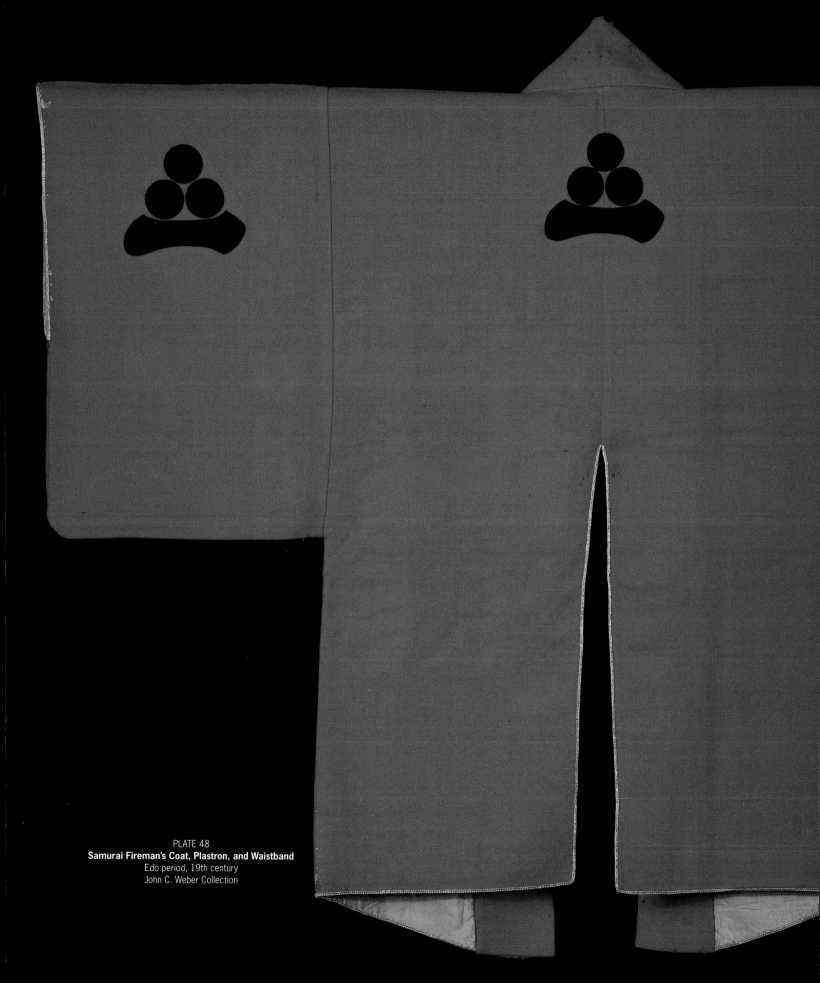

PLATE 48
Samurai Fireman's Coat, Plastron, and Waistband
Edo period, 19th century
John C. Weber Collection

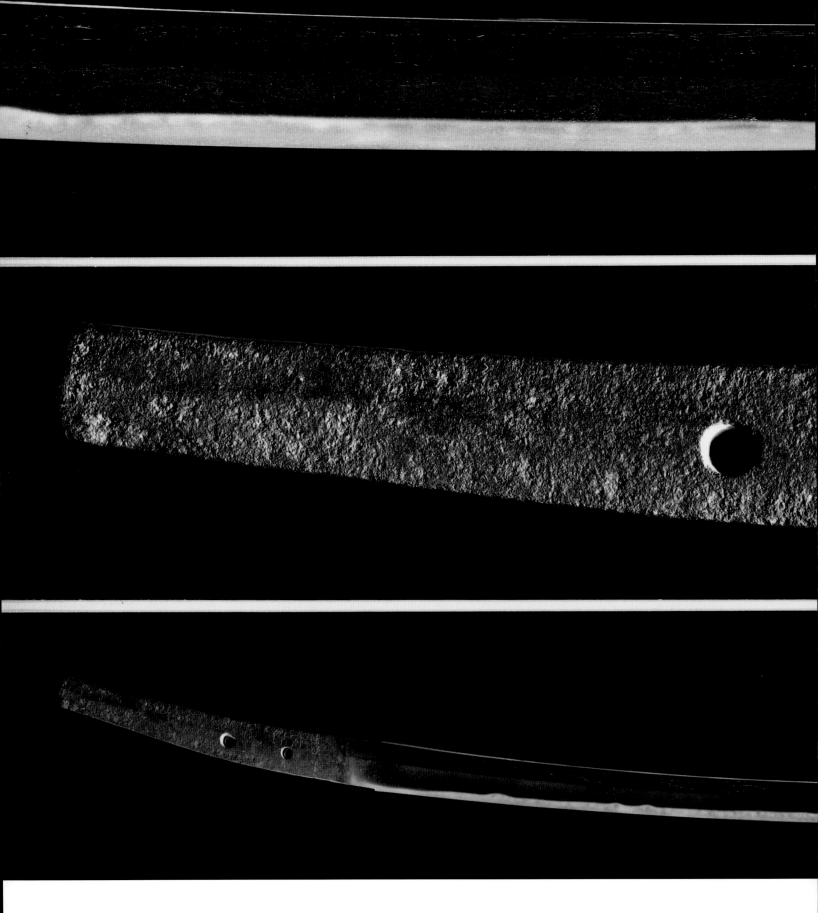

PLATE 49
Sword (*tachi* type, slung cutting edge down)
Kamakura period, late 13th–early 14th century
Museum of Fine Arts, Boston

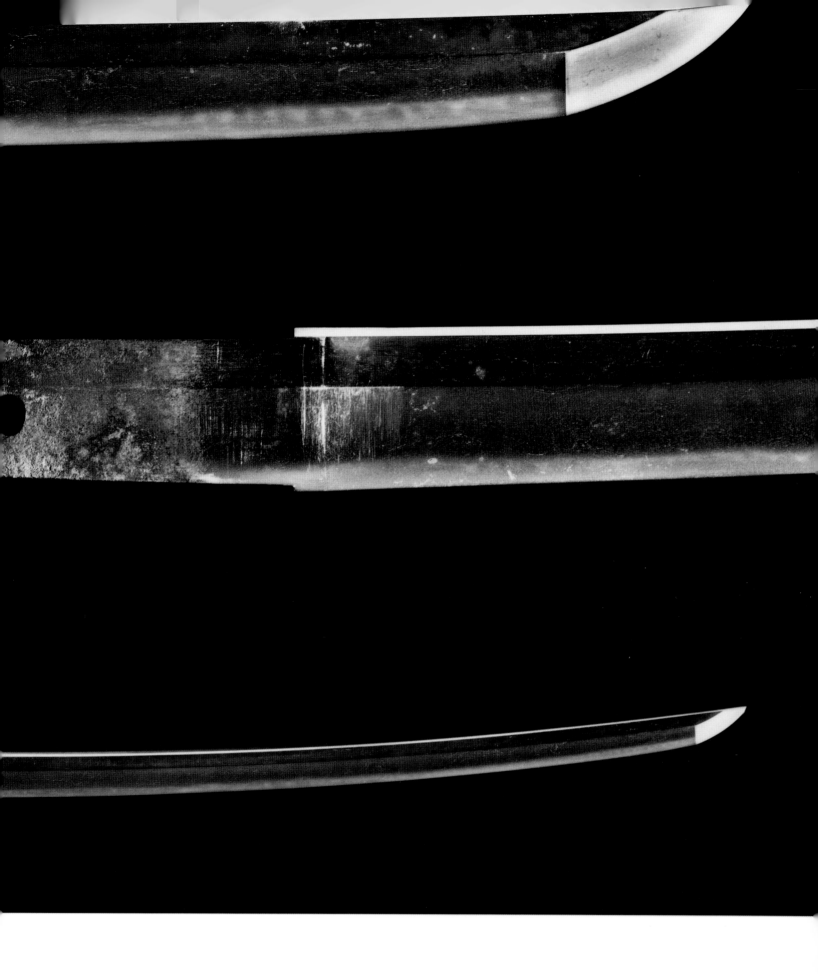

PLATE 50
Sword (*tachi* type, slung cutting edge down) with Mounting (not shown)
Late Kamakura-early Nambokucho period, mid-14th century
Museum of Fine Arts, Boston

PLATE 51
Guardless Sword Mounting with Lacquer Sheath
Momoyama period, late 16th–early 17th century
Private Collection

PLATE 52
Sword Guard
Mid-Edo period, 18th century
Museum of Fine Arts, Boston

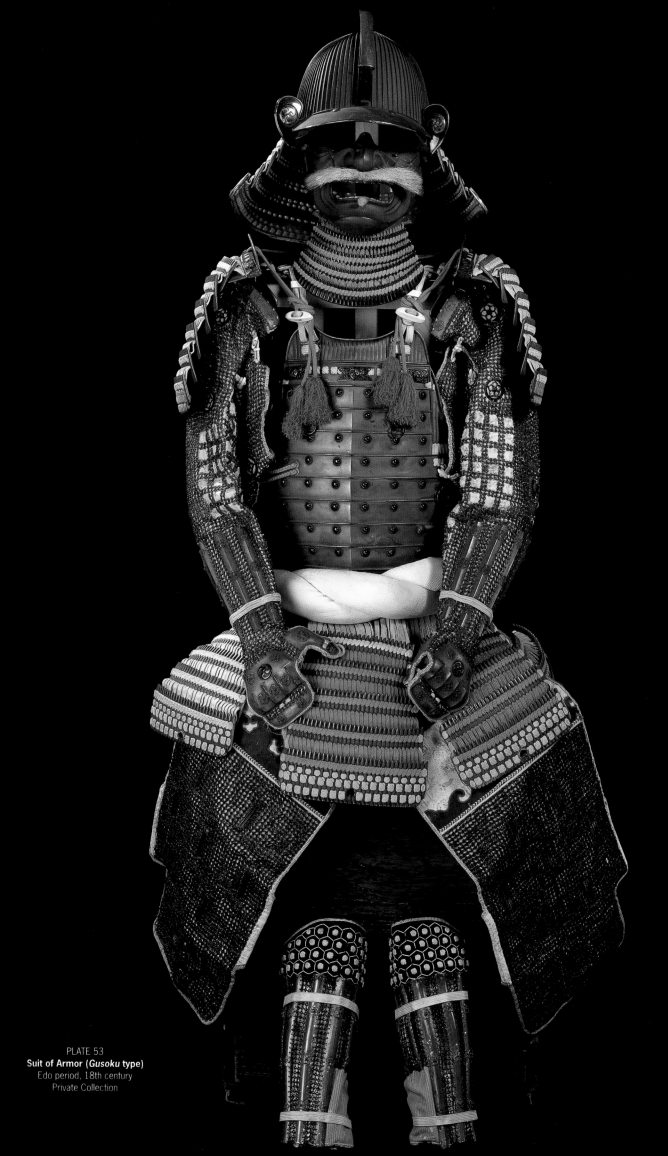

PLATE 53
Suit of Armor (*Gusoku* type)
Edo period, 18th century
Private Collection

PLATE 54
Wash Basin
Momoyama period, early 17th century
John C. Weber Collection

PLATE 55
Jar
Edo period, 18th century
Philadelphia Museum of Art

PLATE 56
Woman's *Kosode* Robe
Edo period, late 17th century
Philadelphia Museum of Art

Plate 57
Woman's *Kosode*
Edo period, early 19th century
John C. Weber Collection

PLATE 58
Woman's *Kosode* Robe
Edo period, early 19th century
Philadelphia Museum of Art

126

PLATE 59
Writing Box and Table
Meiji period, late 19th–early 20th century
The Florence and Herbert Irving Collection

PLATE 60
Pair of Sake Bottles
Momoyama period, late 16th century
Peggy and Richard M. Danziger Collection

PLATE 61
Covered Dish
Edo period, early 18th century
Philadelphia Museum of Art

PLATE 62
Set of *Mukōzuke* Dishes
Momoyama period, late 16th–early 17th century
Peggy and Richard M. Danziger Collection

PLATE 63
Tea Bowl
Momoyama period, early 17th century
Peggy and Richard M. Danziger Collection

PLATE 64
Three-tiered Food Box
Edo period, 17th century
Peggy and Richard M. Danziger Collection

EDO CHIC

粋 Iki

Edo Chic

Iki

In iki *there had to be Edo's "plucky chic" and the "chivalry of South East Edo."*
There had to be unimpeachable refinement and dignity in common between
"smartness," "dash," and "affected bravado."

Kuki Shūzō, *The Structure of Iki* (1930) [1]

I KI TASTE IS WORLDLY and absolutely urban. It is an elusive concept; the translation of "cool" and "chic" hint at its nuances but miss the undertones of its cultural derivation. *Iki* is intrinsically associated with the world of the wealthy merchants and pleasure-seeking citizens of Edo (present-day Tokyo), Osaka, and Kyoto during the latter half of the Edo period (1615–1868). It is a sensibility of coquettish fashion, how certain styles of clothing and accessories are carried off—an aesthetic taste *par excellence.* Imagine a rake headed for a night in the pleasure quarters wearing a smart kimono with some daring but successful pattern, or a subtle weave that the knowing eye would recognize for its outrageous cost. Or visualize a member of the many city guilds: a fireman kitted out in the kind of festival costume that could only be worn successfully with a bit of bravado, the certain swagger that identified a local hero. The opposite of *iki* is *yabo*, meaning churlish, unstylish, and lacking in street smarts or boringly conventional, as in our sense of being "square."

To some extent *iki* taste was subversive, and to understand why it is necessary to consider the social milieu of the time. Under the Tokugawa shogunate's system of social classes that placed samurai and farmers above artisans and merchants, the term *chōnin* (literally, townspeople) referred to those city-dwellers engaged in a broad range of trade, financial services, labor, and handicraft. While in theory the military-administrative group was the highest social class, distinctions were breaking down as interregional trade and commerce flourished, propelling the merchants into higher and higher strata of wealth. While they luxuriated in the good but expensive life of cities like Kyoto, Osaka, and Edo, the daimyo and samurai became gradually impoverished.

The Tokugawa shogunate, concerned about upstart trends in the extravagant display of wealth among the merchant class, prescribed sumptuary laws to regulate their consumption of expensive goods, including clothing and accessories. *Iki* arose in part to subvert and game those sumptuary laws by devising designs that looked humble but were, in fact, lavishly expensive. The *chōnin* would line their clothing, restricted by code to cotton or plain silk, with sumptuous materials. Rather than displaying the bold and brightly colored robes favored by the nobility, *iki* connoisseurs promoted the fashion of subdued colors and small, geometric stencil patterns that, on close inspection, were as fine as the most elaborate court costumes. Accessories, including inro and smoking sets (Plates 72, 73, 76), that used exotic, imported materials or imitated lowly materials with a highly skilled deployment of lacquer and inlay techniques, such as those designed by the Edo lacquer artist, Shibata Zeshin (1807–1891) became chic and fashionable among the urban merchant class.

Iki taste was also defined by the codes of the pleasure quarters. In pre-modern Edo, the pleasure quarters comprised a city-within-a-city where a highly sophisticated punctilio had evolved that was much at odds with that observed outside the gates. Members of the highest social ranks were not supposed to be seen near the place, and if they went at all it was usually in disguise; visiting samurai were obliged to check their swords upon arrival. Once inside the gates, the divisions of social rank broke down, and men found themselves on a level playing field competing for courtesans' favors. In contrast, the courtesans were ranked very carefully according to their beauty, entertainment skills, and talent at handling men; the highest ranking *(oiran)* were treated like princesses within the quarter.

For the visiting rake, showering extravagant and regular largess went without question—the bill would come soon enough—but much more than cash was needed to catch the eye of one of the ranking courtesans. Good looks and vigor certainly helped, but stylish attire, charm, debonair manners, amusing conversation, and persistence went along with the price. The collector and connoisseur Goke Tadaomi has written, "*iki* [is] light and unconstrained, gallant without being obstinate, playful but never tiresome, assertive but not argumentative, standing on one's honor and thinking nothing of one's own safety, standing on the side of the weak against the strong."[2] It was in such a world, which also included the other Edo pleasures of Kabuki theater and the grand spectacle of sumo wrestling, that *iki* taste evolved.

The early modern philosopher and aesthete, Kuki Shūzō (1888–1941), explored the world of Edo chic in his influential book of 1930, *Reflections on Japanese Taste: The Structure of Iki*. A cosmopolitan member of the modernizing elite in Japan, he studied in Europe under Husserl and was acquainted with Heidegger, Bergson, and Sartre. Kuki was one of the first Japanese thinkers to forge a Japanese aesthetic, bridging European and Japanese traditions in philosophy. What its protagonists, the Edo pleasure-seeker and his paramours, would have made of Kuki's analysis of *iki* can only be imagined, but to catch even a whiff of *iki* taste, which was such a fascinating element of Edo life, is worth the effort.

According to Kuki, relationships between members of the opposite sex form the ethos of *iki*, particularly as manifested in coquetry and its many artful devices. *Iki* is seen in the affectation of a certain resistance to and disdain of the opposite sex, which cause tensions that inspire the pursuer to greater efforts, only until conquest has been realized. He compliments the "brave composure," even chivalry, of the *otokodate,* a heroic outlaw who like Robin Hood robbed the rich to give to the poor, or the fireman who wore only the uniform of his guild (*kajibanten*) and went out in his white socks alone in defiance of the winter cold, as ideals "alive with vitality" and characteristic of *iki*. The self-composed warrior employing a toothpick as if he had just eaten, when in fact he was starving, or the Edoite's pride in blowing his last funds in the pleasure quarter without a thought for the next day's promise of bankruptcy are forms of resignation iconic of *iki* and consistent with Buddhist fatalism, being alive in the here-and-now, with no concern for the future. The bittersweet quality of *iki* reflects awareness that beauty is only fleeting—a ruling precept of the pleasure quarter.

Retaining this domain as the measure of *iki*, Kuki describes the "graceful elegance" of a heart that has "gone through the polishing of the hard and heartless floating world." He evokes the image of a courtesan, still beautiful but with the bloom of youth fading, and observes: "Once you have set eyes on the vague traces of warm and sincere tears behind a bewitching, lightly-worn smile, you will have been able to grasp the manifestation of *iki* for the first time. Perhaps the resignation in *iki* is a mood produced by over-ripeness and decadence."

Although it is manifested in countless nuances of countenance, dress, and movement, the *iki* pose is slightly disordered but always presumes a slender, willowy figure as seen in the prints of the ukiyo-e artists Kitagawa Utamaro, Torii Kiyonaga, and Katsukawa Shun'ei, who assiduously studied the habitués of the Edo demimonde. Parallel vertical stripes express the *iki* ideal in dress, while horizontal stripes and checks are best only as a form of contrast, such as a striped sash breaking the vertical pattern of the kimono. The choice and combination of such subtle colors as mouse gray (*nezumi-iro*), tea brown (*kobicha*), yellowish brown (*kigaracha*), indigo blue (*kon*), and grayish blue (*nando*) reinforce the *iki* aesthetic. Fine examples of these patterns, like the bold-striped kimono (Plate 67) and grayish kimono with small stencil design (Plate 68), represent the essence of *iki* taste in fashion.

Ascribing objects of everyday use to the canons of Edo Chic is a less exact exercise, but the daring and unconventional styles of the wealthy merchant class did manifest themselves in certain preferred patterns of ceramic and lacquer design. Geometric patterns, as in a superb set of Arita dishes displaying a zigzag checkered design (Plate 79), were especially *iki*. Lacquer accessories such as a wooden sword by Shibata Zeshin, which is made to look like rotting wood but is in fact a work of high lacquer craftsmanship, expressed the perfect *iki* conceit of artistic deceit (Plate 77). Finally, the shop signs (*kanban*) whose cunning designs helped the urban merchant class vie for customers or those signs for the havens of the *iki* set—the kabuki theater and teahouse (euphemism for pleasure house)—are also marks of Edo life that compose the ephemeral joys of "the floating world."

1. Kuki Shūzō, *Reflections on Japanese Taste: The Structure of Iki*. Translated by John Clark (Sydney: Power Publications, 1997), p. 40. Originally published in Japanese in 1930.

2. Goke Tadaomi quoted in Joe Earle and Goke Tadaomi, *Meiji no Takara: Treasures of Imperial Japan: Masterpieces by Shibata Zeshin* (Tokyo: The Kibo Foundation, 1996), p. 28.

The Actor Ichikawa Monnosuke II as Karigone Bunshichi
The Actor Sakata Hangoro II
Katsukawa Shunshō (1726-1793)
Edo period, dated 1780
Color woodcut, *hosoban*
Brooklyn Museum of Art, Museum Collection Fund (16.553, 16.554)

PLATE 65
Townsman's Coat
Edo period, 19th century
Resist-patterned smoked leather
109.9 x 134 cm
John C. Weber Collection

Reversible leather coats made of thick smoked leather (*fusube-gawa*) were worn by high-ranking firefighters, carpenters, and merchants in Edo-period Japan. The technique of smoking leather was apparently introduced to Japan from India in the mid-sixteenth century and was used to impart color as well as to "cure" the leather, rendering it water-repellant. Depending on the materials used and the duration of smoking, various shades of brown, gray, and blue could be obtained. Rice straw was the common material for smoking, used to produce the deep brown color, like that seen on this jacket. Prior to the smoking, wax or gum was applied through a stencil, creating a pattern reserved in white on the smoked leather ground.

The large crest on the upper back reads "House of Yoshi." Yoshi is likely the first part of a surname that, when combined with two or three additional characters, would make up the name to which the wearer of this coat was affiliated. The geometric design on the lower half also reads "Yoshi" in a stylized script, which was often used as a decorative element on these coats. Two square crests in the stylized script are repeated on the front lapels. The inside was dyed indigo blue and decorated with the Asano family crest, two crossed-hawk feathers in a banded circle. [A.V.A.]

PLATE 66
Fireman's Coat
Late Edo period, 19th century
Paste resist-dyed plain-weave cotton, quilted
100.3 x 121.9 cm
John C. Weber Collection

Because the wooden buildings common in Edo-period Japan were prone to fires, a good firefighter was highly regarded and given special status in the community. In the early eighteenth century, the Tokugawa shogunate organized firefighters into two ranks—samurai and townsmen. Members of a town brigade wore reversible, multilayered quilted coats like this one, with matching hood, gloves, and trousers. These ensembles, called *kajibanten*, identified the commoner firemen, who were romanticized as dashing, daring, tough-guy heroes. Although these uniforms were soaked in water and worn wet for extra protection in fire-fighting—which added as much as eighty pounds to the weight the firefighter carried—few coats survived the hazards of this job in as good condition as this one.

Firemen specially commissioned the dramatic designs on their uniforms to express their pride and bravura. Designs were drawn with the rice paste-resist technique (*tsutsugaki*). A large fire brigade standard (*matoi*), an auspicious symbol to protect the firefighter, is incorporated in this design along with the brigade's name, Motomachi-gumi. These standards, which identified a brigade's territory, stood eight to ten feet high and consisted of a large wooden disc and streamers that indicated the direction of the wind. They were held high from a rooftop by standard bearers who coordinated firefighting efforts. [A.V.A.]

PLATE 67
Woman's Robe
Meiji period, late 19th-early 20th century
Spun silk
101.2 x 148.4 cm
Private Collection

Vertical striped kimono, a craze identified with the cultural phenomenon called *iki*, translated as "chic," "fashionable," or "smart-looking," were de rigueur for the fashion-conscious urbanite in late Edo-period Japan. Stripe designs in various subdued shades—gray, dark blue, and brown—were first worn by kabuki actors and female entertainers of the pleasure quarters.

Iki embodied the changing aesthetic and moral ideals of the nineteenth-century townspeople, merchants, and artisans of Edo (Tokyo). The highest expression of *iki* was in personal style, but it was more than a fleeting fashion trend and expressed a quiet revolt, both social resignation and a rebellious spirit. While wearing a subdued striped kimono, the townsman would don an extravagant accessory to flout the detested sumptuary laws.

Iki fashion trends continued to exert strong influence in early twentieth-century kimono design. As cities swelled with newcomers from the countryside, the demand increased for smart-looking affordable silk kimono; vertical-striped kimono were an emblem of modernity among the fashion-conscious. [A.V.A.]

PLATE 68
Woman's *Kosode* Robe
Late Edo period, 19th entury
Stencil resist-dyed silk crepe
144.8 x 120.7 cm
Private Collection

Unpretentious elegance and hidden luxury were at the heart of the late Edo-period fashion of *iki*. After centuries of ever-tightening government restrictions aimed to curb their excessive display of opulence in dress, the townspeople responded by reversing the fashion pendulum: from the obvious to the subtle, from bright to dark colors, and from big patterns to petite repeats, stripes, and checks. The small motif and grayish blue color used for this garment wonderfully typifies this trend. This new fashion style first became prominent among popular kabuki actors and women of the pleasure quarters in the late eighteenth century, and was soon adopted by urban men and women in equal measure.

One motif on this kimono is a repeat design of three opened fan shapes arranged in a circle, sometimes overlapping. The pattern was created with a resist-dyeing process, in which rice paste was applied through a stencil, which was repositioned repeatedly along the entire length of silk required for the *kosode*. The quality of the finished fabric was determined by the dyer's exacting skills in cutting and positioning the stencil and maintaining the consistency of the paste. [A.V.A.]

PLATE 69
Woman's Summer *Kosode* Robe
Edo period, 19th century
Resist-dyed and painted plain-weave ramie
116.8 x 168.3 cm
John C. Weber Collection

Both the material and the pattern chosen for this unlined summer *kosode* reflect the high humidity and heat characteristic of Japanese summers. Ramie was the preferred fabric for summer robes because of its quick-drying qualities and pleasant texture on the skin. The motif of plovers darting among drying fishing nets along the shore at sunset offers an imaginary respite from the unbearable summer heat of the city. Plovers were associated with the winter season in poetry; patterns with wintry associations were popular for lightweight summer robes, perhaps because they were psychologically cooling. This motif appears in such classical Japanese literature as this thirteenth-century poem by the Buddhist priest Dogen (1234–1304):

> The fishermen's boat
> Had just been beached and tied as
> The evening tide
> Rose and rose, still more and more
> Flocks of plovers are crying

—translation by Andrew J. Pekarik (in Money L. Hickman, et al. *Japan's Golden Age: Momoyama*. Dallas Museum of Art, 1996).

The design along the hem was created with the *yūzen* dyeing method in which rice paste, applied through a cone-shaped tool, produced thin white lines, a hallmark of this intricate process. These white lines form both the outline and some of the details, which can be seen clearly in the pattern of the fishing nets. The poetic mood of early evening at the shore is enhanced by the gradual change of color from pink to gray in the sky above the water, subtle shading created by the *bokashi* technique. Mouse gray (*nezumi iro*) was one of the subdued colors popular for garments among the late Edo-period merchant class.

The crest on this robe, "a crane in a circle," was originally somewhat larger, in the style of the earlier Edo period. As smaller crests became popular in the Meiji period, this kimono was reworked and the size of the crest was reduced. [A.V.A.]

PLATE 70
Woman's Three-quarter–Length Jacket
Taisho period, early 20th century
Tie-dyed figured silk crepe
92.7 x 128.3 cm
John C. Weber Collection

Popular belief holds that the daring geisha of the Fukagawa district located on the outskirts of Edo (Tokyo) were the first women to wear *haori*, originally men's wear, in the late seventeenth century. Wearing *haori* only became fashionable among women of all classes in the late 1890s, but today it is considered an integral part of the kimono ensemble. The lightweight silk and the small yoke indicate that this casual *haori* would have been worn in summer.

The tie-dyed design of weighted cords, casually draped over the shoulders and sleeves of the garment, suggests a beaded door curtain. Several of the ends are looped, creating a sense of movement. Some cords—on both the front and the back—extend beyond the lower hem and playfully wrap around to the underside. The crepe was woven in a subtle design that appears black on black and imitates a resist-dyed *ikat* pattern. This simple, but graphically sophisticated and whimsical design demonstrates the continued influence of late Edo-period *iki* fashion on Japanese textiles of the early twentieth century. [A.V.A.]

PLATE 71
Inro
Style of Ogata Kōrin (1658–1716)
Edo period, 18th–19th century
Gold lacquer with lead and mother-of-pearl inlay; soft-metal *ojime*, silk cord
5.7 x 5.1 cm
Philadelphia Museum of Art, Gift of Mrs. S. Emlen Stokes (1987-25-2 a-e)

Rinpa refers to an artistic movement named after Ogata Kōrin (1658–1716), and perpetuated by his followers throughout the Edo and Meiji periods. Most Rinpa artists were painters, but such early founders as Kōrin and his predecessor, Hon'ami Kōetsu (1558–1637), were accomplished in other areas of creativity including ceramic decoration and lacquer design. During the early and middle Edo period, there was much experimentation in lacquer-working techniques. Because a craftsman must develop a resistance to the toxic properties of the sap, it is not certain whether or not well-born artists such as Korin actually handled the raw material. It is more likely that such artists originated the design of an object and supervised its manufacture.

Inro were made of several chambers joined by a silk cord and were used to hold medicines. These *sagemono,* that is, accessories suspended from the obi sash of a man's kimono, were secured by a netsuke. The lid is held in place with a sliding bead (*ojime*). In this inro, mother-of-pearl inlay of a floral motif create a striking artistic effect.   [M.D.]

PLATE 72
Inro
Shibata Zeshin (1807–1891)
Late Edo-early Meiji period
Gold and dark silver lacquer with polychrome lacquer and scratched details, matching *ojime* and netsuke, silk cord
9.6 x 7 cm
Signed: *Zeshin*
Kay and Tom Edson Collection

Inro originally carried personal seals, which are used as signatures in China, Korea, and Japan, but by the beginning of the eighteenth century these small, chambered boxes more often contained medicines. Inro were suspended from the sash of a man's kimono, attached with a sculptured toggle and perforated bead *(ojime)* on a cord that held the inro components tightly together.

Sumptuary laws severely restricted the lifestyle and dress of the merchant class in Edo, but one could flaunt his wealth by wearing an expensive netsuke and inro. Zeshin, the preeminent and most experimental lacquer artist of his day, was a master of simulating other materials—such as iron or bronze—in lacquer: this inro depicts a gong that appears slightly pitted and rusty in imitation of metal, together with a padded striker. By their expensive quality, but lack of flashy ostentation, his objects epitomize the townsman's sense of *iki* chic. The netsuke, shaped like a rice cake, is decorated with a design of chestnuts in *hiramaki-e* lacquer. [M.D.]

PLATE 73
Smoking Set
Shibata Zeshin (1807–1891)
Late Edo-early Meiji period
Pipe: lacquered wood, iron, gold, silver
Pipe case: gold and black lacquer
Tobacco case: dyed cotton with leather backing, silk cord, staghorn netsuke
Length of pipe case: 19.6 cm
Signed: *Zeshin*
The Florence and Herbert Irving Collection

Small items that could be suspended from an obi sash—called *sagemono* as a category and including netsuke, inro, and pipe cases—represented one of the few areas of individual expression for the Edo merchant whose apparel was restricted by Tokugawa sumptuary laws. Luxurious silks and bright colors were prohibited to the low-ranking merchant class, but in *sagemono* accessories one could reveal a bit of extravagance.

Only the lacquer pipe case bears the signature of Shibata Zeshin but his taste seems to have dictated the selection of materials used in this ensemble. Wood sorrel—a Japanese wildflower—is depicted in gold lacquer applied in gradations to represent the actual colors of the plant, set off by a black background. The pipe stem has been lacquered to imitate tortoiseshell, and the mouthpiece and bowl are decorated with gold oak leaves. The netsuke is hollow-carved with a motif of paulownia flowers and leaves. The tobacco pouch, made of leather covered in an exotic *sarasa*—a printed cotton imported from Southeast Asia—has a clasp in the design of a snail, made of gold, silver, and a gray copper-silver alloy.   [M.D.]

PLATE 74
Tobacco Tray
Edo period, 18th century
Kyoto ware, Ko Kiyomizu type; stoneware, cobalt-blue underglaze and enamels
20 x 16.6 x 18.6 cm
Private Collection

Ceramic wares with overglaze enamel decoration have been produced in Kyoto since the mid-seventeenth century and are identified with that city by the name Kyōyaki. Polychrome enamel decoration had also been developed at the porcelain-producing kilns of Arita in northern Kyushu, and many were exported overseas by the Dutch East Indies Company, based at Deshima Island, just off Nagasaki. Kyōyaki wares, by contrast, were made almost exclusively for the domestic market, and their designs reflect the artistic trends of Kyoto at the time.

This tray was made to present the accoutrements of smoking: a small brazier to hold burning charcoal, a tobacco container, and a pipe or two. The front panel is lower than the back to allow easy access to the items inside. It has been made of stoneware, covered (except for the base) with a transparent glaze that has crackled after the piece was removed from the kiln. It is decorated with a design of gourds in overglaze gold, green, and blue enamels; cutouts in the sides and back echo this charming gourd design.   [M.D.]

PLATE 75
Tobacco Container
Edo period, 19th century
Negoro ware; red lacquer
7 x 6 cm
Peggy and Richard M. Danziger Collection

Traditional Japanese tobacco was very finely shredded and smoked in small quantities—little more than one puff—in a pipe with a tiny bowl. Owners who prided themselves on their selections of sake cups and flasks spent similar attention on collecting and arranging smoking accoutrements. Small, unusual, or finely made objects, which were not overtly ostentatious but had a quality or rarity that would be recognized by the knowing eye, commanded high prices from *iki* dandies and collectors.

This small tobacco container, made in a truncated oval shape with fluted sides, incorporated the *iki* taste for unusual geometric forms. [M.D.]

PLATE 76
Scabbard with Mounting

Shibata Zeshin (1807–1891)
Late Edo-early Meiji period (19th century)
Lacquered wood; fittings: black lacquer with gold and brown lacquer decoration; *menuki*: gilt metal
41.9 x 4.7 x 6 cm
Signed: *Zeshin*
Private Collection

The expensive imitation of ordinary materials and objects in lacquer is both typical of *iki* taste and a technique that Zeshin developed to its apotheosis. The scabbard of this dagger looks like a rotting branch, but all of the details have been carved in great detail to look as natural as possible; a trail of ivy, depicted in colored lacquers, and a clear lacquer finish, complete the effect. The decorations on the grip, sparrows rendered in gold, were made by another craftsman. The rest of the lacquer fittings were all made by Zeshin and continue the theme of trailing ivy in gold and brown lacquer on a polished black ground, adding an elegant complement to the rustic appearance of the scabbard.   [M.D.]

PLATE 77
Ornamental Wooden Sword

Shibata Zeshin (1807–1891)
Late Edo-early Meiji period
Lacquered wood applied with gold and silver lacquer, silver, copper, silk cord
44.3 x 3.8 x 1.2 cm
Signed: *Zeshin*
Private Collection

Imitation swords (*bokuto*), which had no metal blades, were worn tucked in the kimono sash—the same as a real sword—purely as a fashion accessory by those who were not members of the warrior ranks and so were forbidden to carry weapons. This object is very much in *iki* taste as, although it looks like a length of ordinary wood, all of the details of the grain and the bark strip along one side have been cleverly imitated in lacquer. On the handle small inlays of soft metal and lacquer depict twisted-straw festoons (usually seen hanging from shrine gates) on a tray, with a sake cup on one side and a votive picture of a rooster and a hen on the other. One side of the blade is decorated with a design of kitchen utensils in raised lacquer, gold and silver. The other side of the blade has an inscription in raised gold lacquer that translates as: *"Even though you may cook rice three times a day, it often turns out either too hard or too soft—we face many obstacles in this world."* This bittersweet observation reveals the rather jaded view that underlies *iki* sensitivities and echoes the Buddhist concepts of life being transient, illusionary, and all too brief.   [M.D.]

PLATE 78
Five-tiered Food Boxes

Shibata Zeshin (1807–1891)
Late Edo period
Gold *maki-e* on brown and green lacquer, silver, mother-of-pearl inlay
41 x 22.8 x 24.4 cm
Kay and Tom Edson Collection

This stacked lunch box (*jubako*) has five sections, which would have been packed with rice and seasonal delicacies for a splendid picnic. It is a tour de force showing Zeshin's ingenious lacquer techniques in a restrained palette of *iki* colors—green, brown, bronze, gray, and black—with highlights in mother-of-pear inlay. Agrimony flowers, grasses, and vines are depicted, along with a willow tree, stylized waves, and a water wheel: all details that would conjure a scene of the Uji river near Kyoto in late summer.   [M.D.]

PLATE 79
Set of Five *Mukōzuke* Dishes

Edo period, 17th century
Arita ware; porcelain painted with underglaze cobalt-blue
Each approximately 14.7 x 8.8 x 2.2 cm
Private Collection

Porcelain was first made in the Arita area of northern Kyushu in the first quarter of the seventeenth century, after white kaolin clay deposits had been found in the area. Immigrant Korean potters introduced the techniques of building climbing kilns that could be fired to over 1200 degrees Centigrade. At this temperature, the fine silica grains in the clay would melt to form a hard white porcelain that provided an ideal ground for painted decoration. The decoration of Arita porcelains was mainly painted in underglaze cobalt blue; after 1640, colored overglaze enamels were also widely used. Many designs were borrowed from those on Chinese imports and showed naturalistic or mythological subjects, but some were of purely native Japanese inspiration.

By itself, the pattern of square checks in blue-and-white on these dishes is not unique, but this composition shows an advanced sense of space and balance—the pattern is echoed on the shallow square rims of each dish in the form of a solid blue zigzag. This type of clever geometric design was indicative of *iki* taste.   [M.D.]

PLATE 80
Set of Five *Mukōzuke* Dishes

Momoyama period, early 17th century
Mino ware, Oribe type; glazed stoneware, iron-oxide design and copper-green glaze
2.7 x 9 x 5.1 cm
Peggy and Richard M. Danziger Collection

These five *mukōzuke* have twelve vertical and nine horizontal corrugations that were made by using a mold to impress the form. Decoration consists of vertical stripes on one side and a grid of squares with a central dot on the other, painted in underglaze iron-oxide. On each side there is a splash of the typical Oribe copper-green glaze, which was probably applied with a ladle.

Painted Oribe wares of the Momoyama period are noted for expressive designs based on both figurative objects such as flowers and animals, as well as geometric patterns. Although this set was made a little earlier than the time of the Edo townsman, the vertical stripes and geometric design are perfectly consistent with *iki* aesthetic taste. [M.D.]

PLATE 81
Fire Warden's Shop Sign
Meiji period, early 20th century
Wood, pigment
29.2 x 76.3 cm
Private Collection

Firefighters were popular heroes of Japan's cities, where, until modern times, most buildings were made of wood, charcoal fires were used for cooking, and fires were common. Each section of the city had its own firemen's guild identified by a decorative standard (*matoi*), such as those pictured on this sign. A vanguard scout would indicate the location of a blaze by waving his group's *matoi*—which would be mounted on a long pole—from a rooftop where it could be easily seen. This sign would have hung at a central fire station as it shows the ten numbered *matoi* of the groups in its area. The top-right characters indicate the locality of these groups ("Dai-ichi-ku"), and the name of the woodcarver (Hiraiwa) who made the sign is at the bottom right. As the sign of one of Edo Japan's most distinctive figures—the fireman with his swashbuckling costumes for both firefighting and festivals—this sign expresses the taste and times of the Edo-period townsman. [M.D.]

PLATE 82
Plaque for Ichikawa Danjurō, Kabuki Actor
Late Edo-early Meiji period, 19th century
Wood, pigment, metal hook
51 x 20 cm
Peabody-Essex Museum, Gift of E.S. Morse, 1898
(E 4168)

This sign (*kanban*), which was most likely displayed inside a kabuki theater, depicts the actor with the hereditary name Danjūrō in the role of the superhero Kamakura Gongorō Kagemasa in the play *Shibaraku*. The date of this kanban suggests that it was made for Ichikawa Danjūrō IX (1838–1903), who took the name of Danjūrō in 1874. The Ichikawa crest of three nesting *masu* (rectangular wooden rice measures) appears at the top of the sign. On the back there is an inscription that begins, "Kaomise ya...." which refers to the "face-showing" performances of the kabuki's season, held each November. The kabuki theater, along with the sumo ring and the pleasure quarters, were central to the world of the Edo townsman where *iki* style was most evident. [M.D.]

PLATE 83
Teahouse Sign
Edo period, 19th century
Wood, lacquer, shell and ceramic inlay
85 x 71 cm
Peabody-Essex Museum, Gift of C. L. Freer, 1908
(E 12,519)

Teahouses, which were common venues for the arranging of trysts in the pleasure quarters of Edo towns, were identified by signs such as this. The design shows a shrine gate (*torii*), together with a maple tree, and male and female deer. Deer were considered to be messengers from the gods, but in the context of a teahouse sign, perhaps a more earthly meaning can be discerned: a single maple leaf has fallen—hinting at the autumn season—when deer are in rut. [M.D.]

PLATE 84
Box
Koma Kōryūsai (active 18th century)
Mid-Edo period
Wood, polychrome lacquer, metal fittings
22.2 x 28.6 x 23.2 cm
Signed: *Koma Koryūsai* and with cursive monogram
The Metropolitan Museum of Art, Edward C. Moore Collection, Bequest of Edward C. Moore, 1891 (91.1.730)

This box for personal accessories is decorated with forty small medallions, which are identical in size (24 mm) to a type of Japanese pre-modern coin (*tsū-hō*), providing a clue to its function. Both the monetary measure and the size of the box suggest that it was used to store a ledger. Each medallion bears a family crest (*mon*), ornamental emblems used as a form of identification among the imperial family and military elite since the eleventh century.

This box is signed "Koma Kōryū" on the front panel, identifying it with a school of highly skilled lacquer artists who worked for many decades under the patronage of the Tokugawa shogunate. One lacquering technique particular to Koma School artists is gold *maki-e*, a sprinkled pattern over a rich vermilion or black lacquer surface, which is seen on several of the crests decorating this box. [A.V.A.]

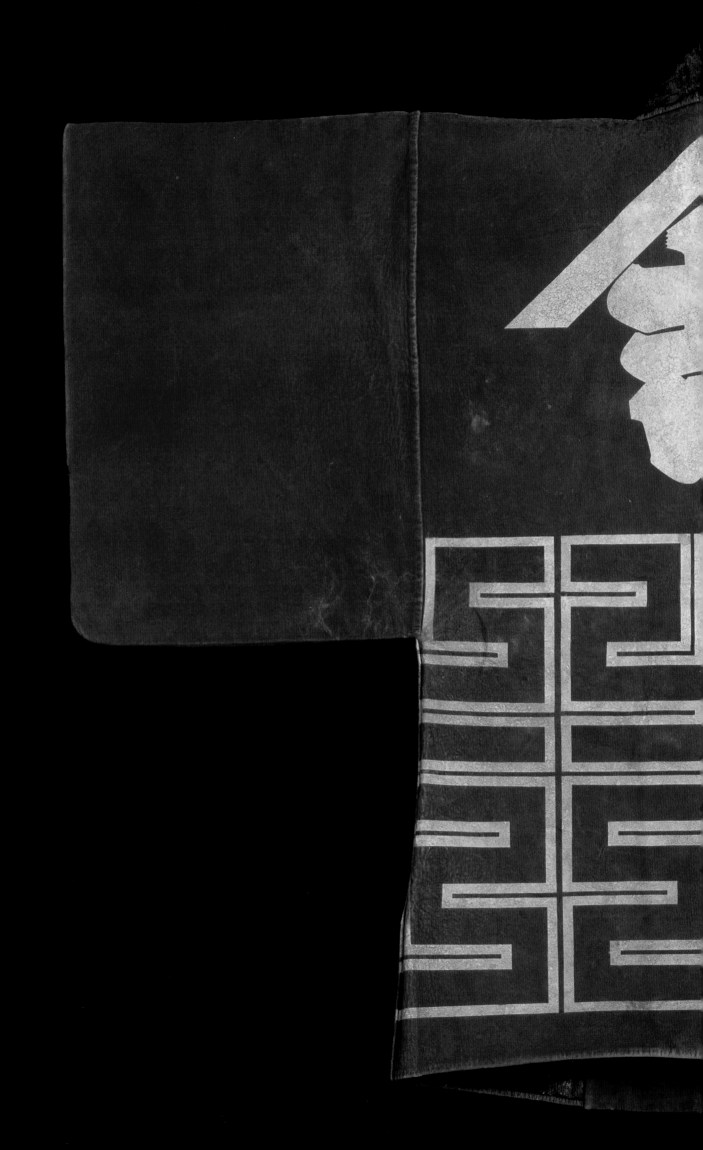

PLATE 65
Townsman's Coat
Edo period, 19th century
John C. Weber Collection

PLATE 66
Fireman's Coat
Late Edo period, 19th century
John C. Weber Collection

PLATE 67
Woman's Robe
Meiji period, late19th-early 20th century
Private Collection

PLATE 68
Woman's *Kosode* Robe
Late Edo period, 19th century
Private Collection

PLATE 69
Woman's Summer *Kosode* Robe
Edo period, 19th century
John C. Weber Collection

PLATE 71
Inro
Edo period, 18th-19th century
Philadelphia Museum of Art

PLATE 72
Inro
Late Edo–early Meiji period
Kay and Tom Edson Collection

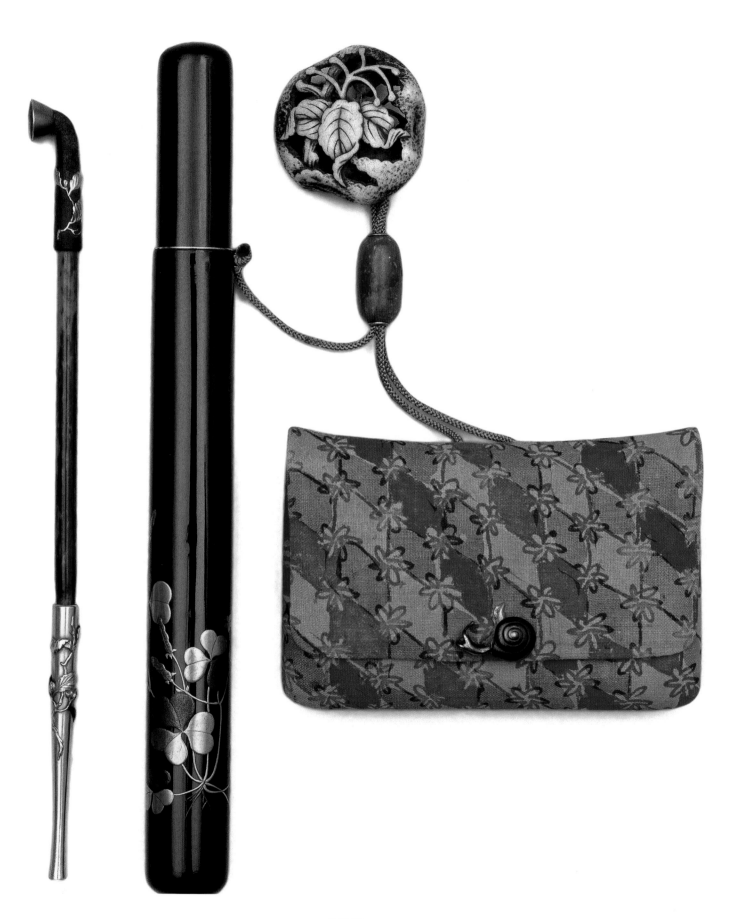

PLATE 73
Smoking Set
Late Edo-early Meiji period
The Florence and Herbert Irving Collection

PLATE 74
Tobacco Tray
Edo period, 18th century
Private Collection

PLATE 75
Tobacco Container
Edo period, 19th century
Shown at left with a rice measure used as a tobacco tray
and a sake cup washer used for ashes (see page 179)
Peggy and Richard M. Danziger Collection

PLATE 76
Scabbard with Mounting
Late Edo-early Meiji period, 19th century
Private Collection

PLATE 77
Ornamental Wooden Sword
Late Edo-early Meiji period
Private Collection

PLATE 78
Five-tiered Food Box
Late Edo period
Kay and Tom Edson Collection

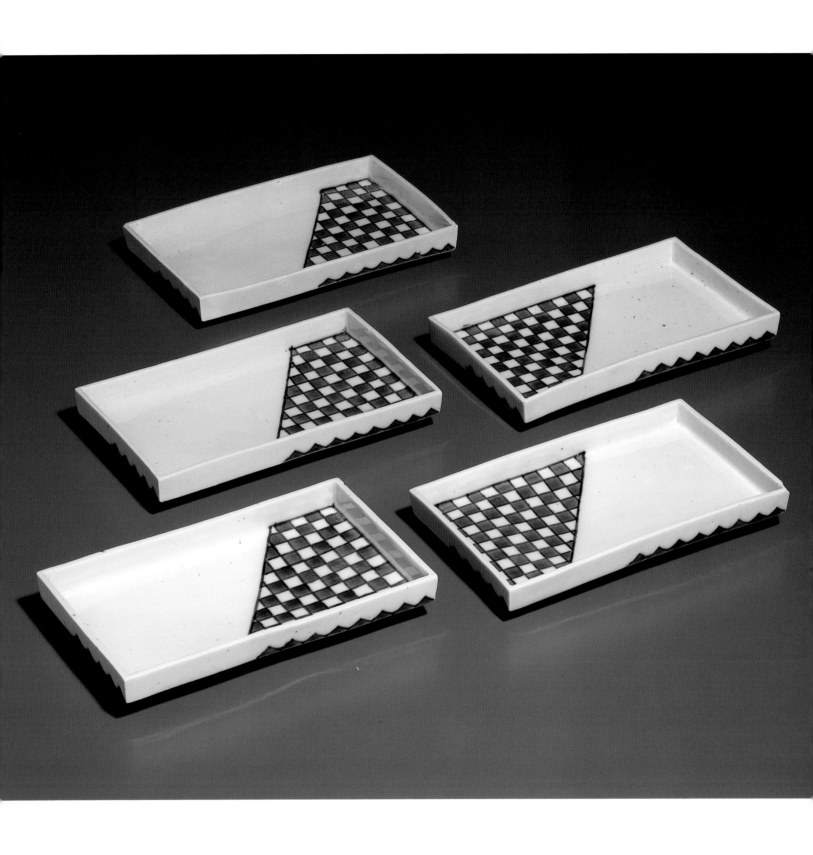

PLATE 80
Set of Five *Mukōzuke* Dishes
Momoyama period, early 17th century
Peggy and Richard M. Danziger Collection

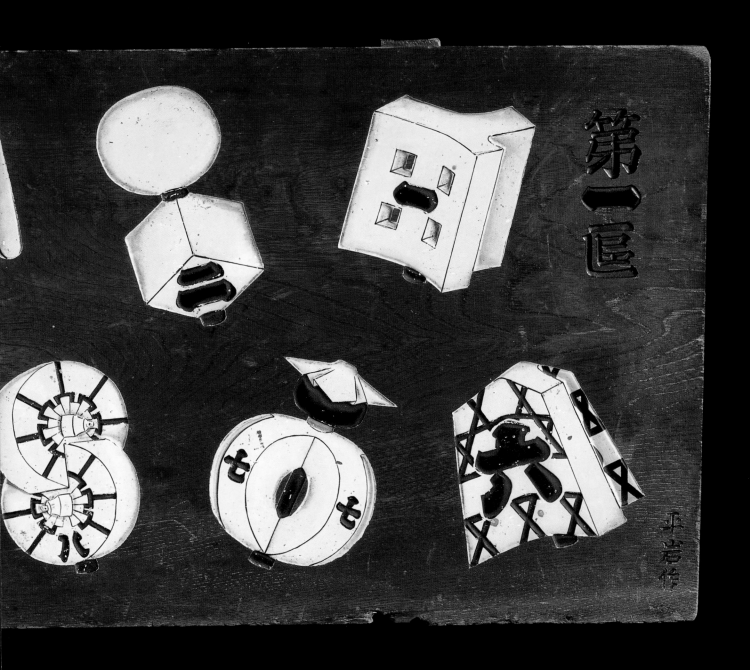

PLATE 81
Fire Warden's Shop Sign
Meiji period, early 20th century
Private Collection

PLATE 82
Plaque for Ichikawa Danjurō, Kabuki Actor
Late Edo-early Meiji period, 19th century
Peabody-Essex Museum

PLATE 83
Teahouse Sign
Edo period, 19th century
Peabody-Essex Museum

PLATE 84
Box
Mid-Edo period, 18th century
The Metropolitan Museum of Art

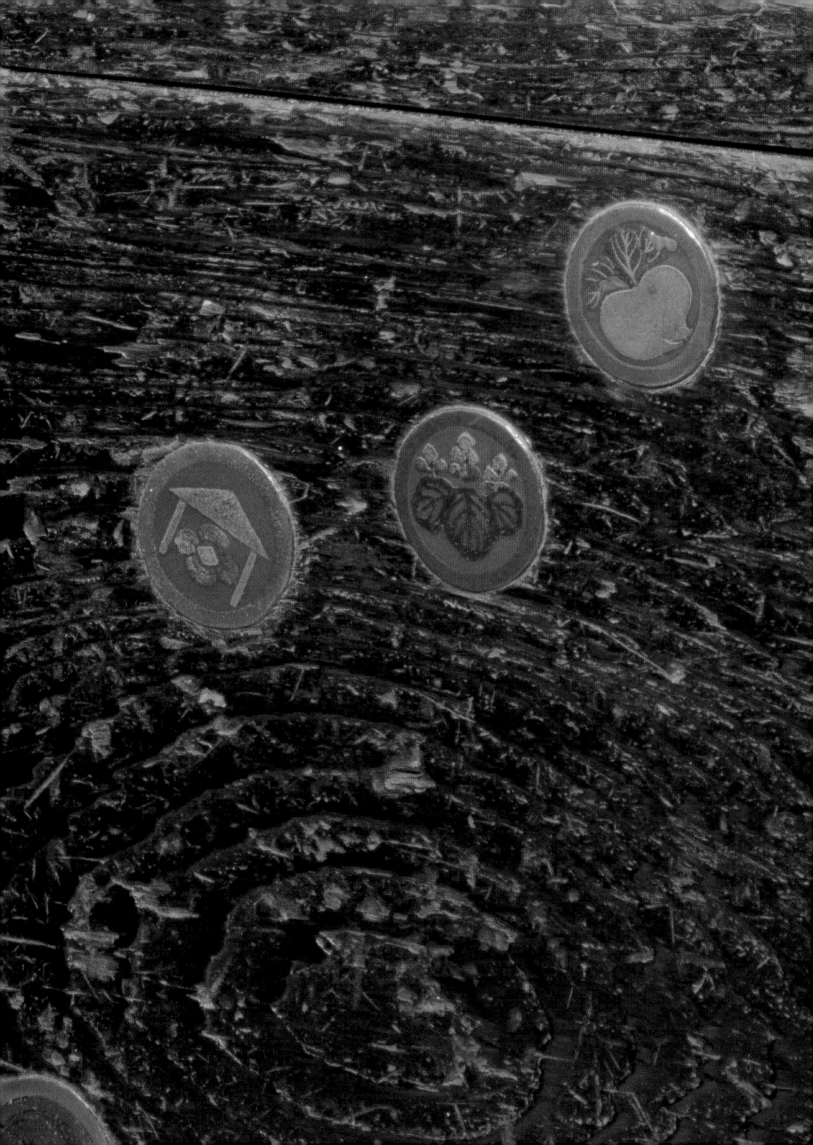

Exhibition Checklist

ANCIENT TIMES: *Kodai no bi*

Large Vessel
Mid Jōmon period, 1500–200 B.C.E.
Earthenware
Height: 60 cm
Collection of LongHouse Reserve, East Hampton,
NY. Purchased with Larsen Fund, 1999

Horned and Stemmed Ax
Mid-late Yayoi period, 1st–3rd century C.E.
Basalt
Length: 25.4 cm
The Metropolitan Museum of Art, The Harry G. C.
Packard Collection of Asian Art, Gift of Harry G. C.
Packard, and Purchase, Fletcher, Rogers, Harris
Brisbane Dick, and Louis V. Bell Funds, Joseph
Pulitzer Bequest, and The Annenberg Fund Inc. Gift,
1975 (1975.268.264)
PLATE 4

Polished Ax
Late Jōmon period, c. 2000–1000 B.C.E.
Serpentine
Length: 15.9 cm
The Metropolitan Museum of Art, The Harry G. C.
Packard Collection of Asian Art, Gift of Harry G. C.
Packard, and Purchase, Fletcher, Rogers, Harris
Brisbane Dick, and Louis V. Bell Funds, Joseph
Pulitzer Bequest, and The Annenberg Fund Inc. Gift,
1975 (1975.268.265)
PLATE 3

Jar on Pedestal
Yayoi period, c. 2nd–4th century C.E.
Earthenware with red pigment
24.4 x 28.3 cm
The Metropolitan Museum of Art, The Harry G. C.
Packard Collection of Asian Art, Gift of Harry G. C.
Packard, and Purchase, Fletcher, Rogers, Harris
Brisbane Dick, and Louis V. Bell Funds, Joseph
Pulitzer Bequest, and The Annenberg Fund Inc. Gift,
1975 (1975.268.379)

Jar
Middle Yayoi period, c. 1st century C.E.
Earthenware with smoke blackening, brushed
surface and appliqué buttons
27.7 x 15.8 cm
Brooklyn Museum of Art, Gift of Carl H. De Silver, by
exchange and the Oriental Art Acquisitions Fund
(74.26.1)
PLATE 6

Jar
Nara period, 7th –8th century C.E.
Sue ware; gray stoneware with natural-ash glaze
25.7 x 25.4 cm
Brooklyn Museum of Art, Frank L. Babbott Fund,
Henry L. Batterman Fund, Contribution fund,
Caroline A. L. Pratt Fund, and the Charles Steward
Smith Memorial Fund

Stand with Attached Miniature Vessels
Attributed to late Kofun period, 6th–7th century C.E.
Sue ware; gray stoneware with natural-ash glaze
Height: 16.5 cm
Brooklyn Museum of Art, Gift of Mrs. Albert H. Clay-
burgh in memory of her mother, Mrs. E. Evelyn Dorr
(66.33)
PLATE 5

Wheel-shaped Bracelet
Early Kofun period, late 3rd–early 4th century C.E.
Steatite
1.3 x 8.9 cm
The Metropolitan Museum of Art, The Harry G. C.
Packard Collection of Asian Art, Gift of Harry G. C.
Packard, and Purchase, Fletcher, Rogers, Harris
Brisbane Dick, and Louis V. Bell Funds, Joseph
Pulitzer Bequest, and The Annenberg Fund Inc. Gift,
1975 (1975.268.388)
PLATE 2

ARTLESS SIMPLICITY: *Soboku*

Spouted Bowl
Edo period, 18th century
Wajima ware; red lacquer
21 x 36 x 26 cm
Jeffrey Montgomery Collection (MC 180)
PLATE 7

Kneading Basin
Edo period, 19th century
Paulownia wood
13 x 80 cm
Jeffrey Montgomery Collection (MC 217)
PLATE 8

Fulling Mallet and Block
Edo period, 19th century
Wood Mallet: 23 x 11 cm; block: 14.5 x 24 cm
Jeffery Montgomery Collection (MC 218.1-.2)
PLATE 9

Kettle Hanger
Late Edo-early Meiji period, 19th century
Zelkova wood
47 x 40 x 20.5 cm
Jeffrey Montgomery Collection (MC 212)
PLATE 10

Kettle Hanger Adjusters
Late Edo-early Meiji period, 19th century
Zelkova wood
Left: 9.5 x 30.3 x 6 cm
Right: 12.5 x 37.5 x 6 cm
Jeffrey Montgomery Collection (MC 124.1-.2)
PLATE 11

Kettle Hanger Adjuster
Edo period, 19th century
Zelkova wood
5 x 30.5 x 3.5 cm
Jeffrey Montgomery Collection (MC 711)

Kettle Hanger Adjuster
Edo period, 18th century
Wood, black lacquer
8 x 30 x 3.5 cm
Jeffrey Montgomery Collection (MC 123)J

Cooking Vessel
Edo period, 19th century
Cast iron, red lacquer lid
9 x 26.3 cm
Jeffrey Montgomery Collection (MC 199)
PLATE 12

Tea Kettle
Edo period, 19th century
Cast iron
17.5 x 12.5 cm
Jeffrey Montgomery Collection (MC 198)

Tea Kettle
Meiji period, late 19th century
Cast iron, bronze lid ring
20 x 18 cm
Jeffrey Montgomery Collection (MC 437)
PLATE 13

Sake Pourer
Meiji period, late 19th-early 20th century
Cast iron, copper handle, bronze lid
15.5 x 14.5 cm
Jeffrey Montgomery Collection (MC 465)

Kiln Palette
Meiji-Taisho period, early 20th century
Wood
101 x 38 x 3 cm
Peggy and Richard M. Danziger Collection

Ship's Sake Container
Momoyama period, 16th–17th century
Bizen ware; stoneware with natural-ash glaze
30 x 28 cm
Jeffrey Montgomery Collection (MC 702)
PLATE 14

Sake Bottle
Edo period, 19th century
Fujina ware; glazed stoneware with iron-oxide and
white ash glaze
Height: 25 cm
Jeffrey Montgomery Collection (MC 481)
PLATE 15

Sake Bottle
Late Momoyama-early Edo period, 17th century
Bizen ware; stoneware
Height: 29 cm
Victor and Takako Hauge Collection
PLATE 16

Sake Bottle
Edo period, 19th century
Shodai ware; glazed stoneware with incised design
Height: 15.5 cm
Jeffrey Montgomery Collection (MC 405)

Spouted Beaker
Edo period, 17th century
Hizen ware, Karatsu type; glazed stoneware
9.3 x 17.8 cm
Museum of Fine Arts, Boston, Morse Collection, Gift
by Contribution (92.3105)
PLATE 17

Soba Cups
Edo period, 18th century
Arita ware; glazed porcelain
Height of each approximately 6.6 cm
Brooklyn Museum of Art, Gift of Greg and Natalie
Fitz-Gerald (1996.1.1-.5)
PLATE 18

Incense Burner
Edo period, early 19th century
Arita ware; glazed porcelain
7.6 x 10.6 cm
Peggy and Richard M. Danziger Collection

Large Dish
Edo period, 17th century
Yatsushiro ware; glazed stoneware with incised design
11.5 x 42 cm
Jeffrey Montgomery Collection (MC 330)
PLATE 19

Basket
Late Edo–early Meiji period, 19th century
Birch bark, rope with bone toggle
19.3 x 17.5 x 10.5 cm
Jeffrey Montgomery Collection (MC 226)
PLATE 20

Winnower
Late Meiji-early Taisho period, 20th century
Woven split bamboo
20 x 53 x 65 cm
Jeffrey Montgomery Collection (MC 229)
PLATE 21

Oil Dish
Edo period, 18th–19th century
Seto ware; glazed stoneware, iron-oxide design and copper glaze
Diameter: 23 cm
Jeffrey Montgomery Collection (MC 336)
PLATE 23

Oil Dish
Edo period, 18th–19th century
Seto ware; glazed stoneware, iron-oxide design and copper glaze
Diameter: 23 cm
Jeffrey Montgomery Collection (MC 431)

Dish
Edo period, 18th–19th century
Seto ware; glazed stoneware, iron-oxide design
Diameter: 22 cm
Jeffrey Montgomery Collection (MC 600)

Dish
Edo period, 18th–19th century
Seto ware; glazed stoneware, iron-oxide and cobalt-blue design
6.8 x 27 cm
Jeffrey Montgomery Collection (MC 425)
PLATE 22

Dish
Edo period, early 19th century
Seto ware; glazed stoneware, underglaze cobalt-blue design
6.7 x 27.6 cm
The Metropolitan Museum of Art, The Harry G. C. Packard Collection of Asian Art, Gift of Harry G. C. Packard, and Purchase, Fletcher, Rogers, Harris Brisbane Dick, and Louis V. Bell Funds, Joseph Pulitzer Bequest, and The Annenberg Fund Inc. Gift, 1975 (1975.268.605)

Travel Cape
Edo period, 19th century
Cotton, indigo, paper interlining
100 x 243 cm
Jeffrey Montgomery Collection (MC 700)
PLATE 24

Overcoat
Meiji period, late 19th century
Cotton, indigo, quilting
139.7 x 113.3 cm
The Metropolitan Museum of Art, Purchase, Mrs. Jackson Burke Gift, 1979 (1979.409)
PLATE 25

Storage Jar
Late Momoyama-early Edo period, 17th century
Tamba ware; glazed stoneware
28 x 23 cm
Victor and Takako Hauge Collection

Storage Jar
Momoyama period, 16th –17th century
Tamba ware; stoneware with natural-ash glaze
Height: 27.9 cm
Brooklyn Museum of Art, Anonymous gift (76.185.1)

Tea Storage Jar
Momoyama period, late16th century
Shigaraki ware; stoneware with ash glaze and incised banded design
33 x 22.8 cm
Brooklyn Museum of Art, Gift of Dr. Richard and Mrs. Ruth Dickes (82.219)

Storage Jar
Momoyama period, late 16th century
Iga ware; stoneware with natural-ash glaze
30.5 x 22.8 cm
Philadelphia Museum of Art, The John T. Morris Fund and The John D. McIlhenny Fund (1993-66-1)
PLATE 27

Storage Jar
Muromachi period, 16th century
Tamba ware; stoneware with natural-ash glaze
49 x 40 cm
Jeffrey Montgomery Collection (MC 136)
PLATE 26

ZEN AUSTERITY: *Wabi*

Sake Vessel
Muromachi period, 15th–16th century
Negoro ware; red lacquer
30.5 x 16.6 cm
Brooklyn Museum of Art, Gift of Robert B. Woodward, by exchange and the Oriental Art Acquisitions Fund (74.4)
PLATE 28

Ewer
Muromachi period, late 16th century
Negoro ware; red lacquer and exposed wood
24.1 x 20.3 x 18.4 cm
Brooklyn Museum of Art, Gift of Dr. Hugo Munsterberg (87.129.1 a-b)

Large Bowl
Muromachi period, 16th century
Red lacquer
11.4 x 39.3 cm
Brooklyn Museum of Art, Gift of the Asian Art Council (1989.53)

Kettle, known as *Taya Itome*
Late Muromachi-early Momoyama period, 16th century
Cast iron, bronze lid
17.5 x 13.5 x 29 cm
Peggy and Richard M. Danziger Collection
PLATE 29

Brazier
Tsuji Seimei (b. 1927)
Showa period, late 20th century
Shigaraki ware; stoneware
23 cm x 44 cm
Signed: *Tsu*
Peggy and Richard M. Danziger Collection

Pair of Kettle Handles
Edo period, 17th century
Iron with silver inlay
Diameter of each: 7.8 cm
Peggy and Richard M. Danziger Collection

Water Jar in Shape of Well Bucket
Muromachi period, 15th century, with later additions
Iron, lacquered interior, pewter lid
27.9 x 12.7 cm
Peggy and Richard M. Danziger Collection

Tea Bowl
Momoyama period, early 17th century
Shigaraki ware; stoneware with natural-ash glaze
9.7 x 8.3 cm
Peggy and Richard M. Danziger Collection
PLATE 33

Tea Bowl
Edo period, 18th century
Red Raku ware; glazed earthenware
5.5 x 13.8 cm
Peggy and Richard M. Danziger Collection
PLATE 32

Tea Caddy
Nakamura Sōtetsu, active early 20th century
Black lacquer
6.5 x 6.6 cm
Peggy and Richard M. Danziger Collection

Tea Scoop, called *Amanogawa* (Milky Way)
Hatakeyama Seiji (1922–1988)
Bamboo
Length: 18 cm
Peggy and Richard M. Danziger Collection

Incense Box
Muromachi period, 16th century
Gold on brown lacquer with metal rim
3 x 4.7 x 3.8 cm
Peggy and Richard M. Danziger Collection

Flower Basket
Early Showa period, dated 1927
Woven bamboo
27.9 x 38.1 cm
Peggy and Richard M. Danziger Collection
PLATE 37

Charcoal Basket
Meiji period, late 19th–early 20th century
Woven bamboo, cane
12 x 25 cm
Peggy and Richard M. Danziger Collection
PLATE 34

Charcoal Tongs
Meiji period, late 19th–early 20th century
Iron with silver inlay
Length of each: 26 cm
Peggy and Richard M. Danziger Collection

Water Jar
Late Muromachi period, 16th century
Shigaraki ware; stoneware with natural-ash glaze, black lacquer lid
20 x 17.7 cm
Peggy and Richard M. Danziger Collection
PLATE 30

Tea Bowl
Momoyama period, 16th –17th century
Mino ware, Black Oribe type; glazed stoneware
8.4 x 17 x 13.8 cm
Private Collection
PLATE 31

Hanging Flower Basket
Hayakawa Shōkosai II (1860–1905)
Meiji period
Woven rattan, wood
24.1 x 17.1 x 8.9 cm
Lloyd and Margit Cotsen Collection
PLATE 36

***Mukōzuke* Dish**
Momoyama period, early 17th century
Mino ware, Oribe type; glazed stoneware with iron
slip, underglaze iron painting, and copper glaze
9.5 x 8.4 cm
Brooklyn Museum of Art, Gift of Robert B.
Woodward (03.87)
PLATE 38

Set of *Mukōzuke* Dishes
Edo period, late 18th–early 19th century
Kyoto ware, attributed to Omuro kiln; glazed
stoneware, iron-oxide design
4.5 x 11 x 7 cm
Peggy and Richard M. Danziger Collection
PLATE 39

Two-tiered Food Box
Momoyama period, 17th century
Mino ware, Shino type; glazed stoneware, iron-oxide
design
14 x 15 x 15 cm
Victor and Takako Hauge Collection
PLATE 40

Plate
Momoyama period, late 16th–early 17th century
Mino ware, Gray Shino type; glazed stoneware, iron
slip, incised design
22.4 x 19.6 cm
Peggy and Richard M. Danziger Collection
PLATE 41

Sake Bottle
Momoyama period, late 16th century
Mino ware, Oribe type; stoneware, iron-oxide design
on slip-covered body, copper green glaze
17.8 x 9.5 cm
Asia Society, The Mr. and Mrs. John D. Rockefeller
3rd Collection (1979.227)
PLATE 43

Sake Cup
Momoyama period, early 17th century
Hagi ware; stoneware with white slip brushed on
under clear glaze
4.3 x 6.2 cm
Peggy and Richard M. Danziger Collection
PLATE 44

Sake Cup
Edo period, 17th century
Hizen ware, Karatsu type; glazed stoneware with
gold lacquer repair
Height of each: 3 cm; diameter of each: 2. 5 cm
Peggy and Richard M. Danziger Collection

Tray
Muromachi period, 16th century
Negoro ware; red lacquer
4.5 x 36.3 x 18 cm
Peggy and Richard M. Danziger Collection

Vase
Muromachi period, 16th century
Bronze
24.8 x 8.5 x 5.2 cm
Peggy and Richard M. Danziger Collection
PLATE 35

Flower Basket
Attributed to Wada Waichisai II (1877–1933)
Late Meiji-early Showa period
Woven bamboo, rattan
60 x 19.1 x 17.8 cm
Lloyd and Margit Cotsen Collection

Flower Basket
Edo period, 19th century
Bamboo
20.3 x 19.1 cm
The Metropolitan Museum of Art, Edward C. Moore
Collection, Bequest of Edward C. Moore, 1891
(91.1. 2089)

Kasuga Tray
Kamakura-early Muromachi period, 14th century
Negoro ware; red and black lacquer with mother-of-
pearl inlay
37.8 x 28.2 x 4 cm
Peggy and Richard M. Danziger Collection
PLATE 42

GORGEOUS SPLENDOR: *Karei*

Campaign Coat
Edo period, early 19th century
Wool and metallic thread appliqué on wool, lining of
silk and metallic thread lampas
97.8 x 74 cm
John C. Weber Collection
PLATE 45

Campaign Coat
Edo period, mid-19th century
Ink inscription on stencil resist-dyed plain weave silk
with gold leaf
65 x 110 cm
John C. Weber Collection
PLATE 46

Sleeveless Campaign Coat
Edo period, mid-19th century
110 x 101.2 cm
Embroidered inscription in silk on silk satin with
supplementary weft patterning, lining of woven
hemp stenciled in gold leaf and indigo dye
John C. Weber Collection
PLATE 47

**Samurai Fireman's Coat, Plastron, and
Waistband**
Edo period, 19th century
Wool appliqué on wool twill, silk and metallic trim,
plain-weave silk lining
109.2 x 131.4 cm
John C. Weber Collection
PLATE 48

Suit of Armor (*Gusoku* type)
Edo period, 18th century
Lacquered iron, *shakudō*, mail, silk
148.8 x 49.5 cm
Private Collection
PLATE 53

Samurai Hat
Edo period, 19th century
Black lacquer, gilt copper, silk cord
Width: 41.1 cm
Private Collection

Saddle
Edo period, c. 1630
Gold on black lacquer over wood
25.8 x 37.5 x 35.5 cm
Museum of Fine Arts, Boston, Charles Goddard Weld
Collection (11.5831)

Sword with Pair of Sword Mountings
Kunikane (active 17th century)
Edo period, dated 1642
Tempered steel
Length: 71.1; curvature: 1.8 cm
Museum of Fine Arts, Boston, Charles Goddard Weld
Collection (11.5101, 11.5102)

Dagger (*ken* type)
Kamakura period, dated 1309
Tempered steel
Length: 27; width: 2.25 cm
Private Collection

Dagger (*tanto* type) with Mounting
Nobuhide (active 19th century)
Tempered steel
Length: 28.7 cm
Museum of Fine Arts, Boston, Charles Goddard Weld
Collection (11.5152 a,b)

**Sword (*tachi* type, slung cutting edge down)
with Mounting**
Kanemitsu (active 14th century)
Late Kamakura-early Nambokucho period, mid-14th
century
Tempered steel
Length: 70.5; curvature: 1.86 cm
Museum of Fine Arts, Boston, Charles Goddard Weld
Collection (11.5097a,b)
PLATE 50

Sword (*tachi* type, slung cutting edge down)
Nagamitsu (active late 13th–early 14th century)
Kamakura period
Tempered steel
Length: 80.3; curvature: 2.95 cm
Museum of Fine Arts, Boston, Gift of Mrs. Charles
Goddard Weld (13.281)
PLATE 49

**Guardless Sword Mounting with Lacquer
Sheath**
Momoyama period, late 16th–early 17th century
Gold and black lacquer over wood, rayskin, *shakudō*
, copper, silk
Length: 54.9; curvature: 1.9 cm
Private Collection
PLATE 51

Pair of *Menuki*
Iwamoto Kansai (active 19th century)
Late Edo-early Meiji period
Gold
3.6 x 2.6 cm; 3.5 x 2.5 cm
Museum of Fine Arts, Boston, Charles Goddard Weld
Collection (11.5280)

Pair of *Menuki*
Omori Terumitsu (active 19th century)
Late Edo period
Gold
3.6 x 2.6 cm; 3.5 x 2.5 cm
Museum of Fine Arts, Boston, Charles Goddard Weld
Collection (11.5308)

***Kozuka*, *Fuchi* and *Kashira*, and Pair of
*Menuki***
Araki Tōmei (active 19th century)
Late Edo period
Menuki: Gold
3.6 x 1.5 cm; 3.5 x 1.4 cm
Kozuka: Shakudō, gold, copper (*suaka*)
Length: 9.7 cm
Fuchi: Shakudō, gold, copper (*suaka*)
3.7 x 2.3 cm
Kashira: Shakudō, gold, copper (*suaka*)
3.4 x 1.8 cm
Museum of Fine Arts, Boston, Charles Goddard Weld
Collection (11.5353 a+b, 11.5225, 11.23950)

Pair of *Menuki*
Attributed to Ko-Gotō School
Late Muromachi period, 16th century
Gold repoussé
3.6 x 1.5 cm; 3.5 x 1.4 cm
Museum of Fine Arts, Boston, Charles Goddard Weld
Collection (11.5274)

Sword Guard
Arichika (1661–1742)
Mid-Edo period, 18th century
Copper (*suaka*), gold, *shibuichi*, *shakudō*
7.4 x 7.4 cm
Museum of Fine Arts, Boston, Special Chinese and
Japanese Fund (13.2368)
PLATE 52

Pair of Sword Guards
Kansai Ishiguro Koreyoshi (active 19th century)
Late Edo period
Shakudō,, gold, silver, copper (*suaka*)
8.1 x 7.7. cm; 7.7. x 7.2 cm
Museum of Fine Arts, Boston, William Sturgis
Bigelow Collection (11.11709, 11.11710)

Sword Guard
Omori Teruhide (active 18th century)
Edo period
Shibuichi with gold inlay
7.6 x 7.0 cm
Museum of Fine Arts, Boston, Charles Goddard Weld
Collection (11.5454)

Pair of Sword Guards
Goto Mitsuhiro (active 19th century)
Late Edo period
Shakudō, gold
8.3 x 7.8 cm; 7.7 x 7.1 cm
Museum of Fine Arts, Boston, Charles Goddard Weld
Collection (11.5418, 11.5442)

Sword Guard
Attributed to Hayashi (active 17th century)
Edo period
Iron
7.9 x 7.9 cm
Museum of Fine Arts, Boston, Special Chinese and
Japanese Fund (13.2194)

Wash Basin
Momoyama period, early 17th century
Gold and black lacquer, metal fittings
20.3 x 43.7 cm
John C. Weber Collection
PLATE 54

Cosmetic Box
Edo period, late 19th century
Gold, black lacquer
6 x 9.5 cm
The Metropolitan Museum of Art, Bequest of
Stephen Whitney Phoenix, 1881 (81.1.265 a-i)

Incense Burner
Edo period, 17th–19th century
Copper
12.1 x 31.8 cm
The Metropolitan Museum of Art, Gift of Ellen
Barker, 1942 (42.90.26)

Head Rest
Edo period, 18th–19th century
Arita ware, Imari style; porcelain painted with
enamels and gold pigment
21 x 16.5 cm
Asia Society, The Mr. and Mrs. John D. Rockefeller
3rd Collection (1979.233)

Jar
Edo period, 18th century
Arita ware; porcelain painted with underglaze cobalt-
blue and enamels
30.5 x 24.1 cm
Philadelphia Museum of Art, Taylor Fund (1955-10-1)
PLATE 55

Woman's *Kosode* Robe
Edo period, late 17th century
Stencil-dyed and embroidered figured satin silk
119.4 x 158.7 cm
Philadelphia Museum of Art, Gift of Mr. and Mrs.
Rodolphe Meyer de Schauensee (1951-42-1)
PLATE 56

Woman's *Kosode* Robe
Edo period, early 19th century
Embroidered figured satin silk
172.7 x 117.5 cm
John C. Weber Collection
PLATE 57

Woman's *Kosode* Robe
Edo period, early 19th century
Resist-dyed and embroidered silk crepe
149.9 x 121.9 cm
Philadelphia Museum of Art, The S. S. White III and
Vera White Collection (1967-30-321)
PLATE 58

Writing Box and Table
Yukio Setsuyō (d. 1926)
Meiji period, late 19th–early 20th century
Gold lacquer with gold and silver inlay, silver fittings
Box: 24.8 x 22.9 x 5.1 cm
Table: 61 x 36.8 x 12.4 cm
The Florence and Herbert Irving Collection
PLATE 59

Pair of Sake Bottles
Momoyama period, late 16th century
Gold on black lacquer
Height: 20.3 cm
Peggy and Richard M. Danziger Collection
PLATE 60

Covered Dish
Ogata Kenzan (1663–1743)
Edo period, early 18th century
Kenzan ware; glazed stoneware with slip design,
underglaze iron-oxide, cobalt-blue and copper glaze
Signed: *Kenzan*
8.5 x 14.4 cm
Philadelphia Museum of Art, Purchased with John T.
Morris Fund (1980-45-1 a,b)
PLATE 61

Set of *Mukōzuke* Dishes
Momoyama period, late 16th–early 17th century
Mino ware, Yellow Seto type; glazed stoneware,
incised design, touches of iron-oxide and copper
green glaze
Each approximately 6 x 8.4 cm
Peggy and Richard M. Danziger Collection
PLATE 62

Set of Eight Plates
Ogata Kenzan (1663–1743)
Edo period, early 18th century
Kawarake-type stoneware with partial white slip,
design painted in underglaze cobalt-blue and iron-
oxide, with interior partially covered in clear glaze
Diameter of each approximately 11.2 cm
Signed: *Kenzan*
Peggy and Richard M. Danziger Collection

Tea Bowl
Momoyama period, early 17th century
Mino ware, Black Oribe type; glazed stoneware, iron-
oxide design
17.2 x 14 cm
Peggy and Richard M. Danziger Collection
PLATE 63

Ewer
Momoyama period, early 17th century
Mino ware, Oribe type; glazed stoneware, iron-oxide
design
20 x 20 cm
The Metropolitan Museum of Art, Purchase, Friends
of Asian Art Gifts, 1988 (1988.156 a,b)

Set of *Mukōzuke* Dishes
Momoyama period, late 16th–early 17th century
Mino ware, Oribe type; glazed stoneware, iron-oxide
design and copper glaze
9.8 x 5.7 x 5.4 cm
The Metropolitan Museum of Art, The Harry G. C.
Packard Collection of Asian Art, Gift of Harry G. C.
Packard, and Purchase, Fletcher, Rogers, Harris
Brisbane Dick, and Louis V. Bell Funds, Joseph
Pulitzer Bequest, and The Annenberg Fund Inc. Gift,
1975 (1975.268.437-442)

Three-tiered Food Box
Edo period, 17th century
Gold, silver and black lacquer with mother-of-pearl
inlay
19.2 x 13.5 x 15 cm
Peggy and Richard M. Danziger Collection
PLATE 64

EDO CHIC: *Iki*

Townsman's Coat
Edo period, 19th century
Resist-patterned smoked leather
109.9 x 134 cm
John C. Weber Collection
PLATE 65

Fireman's Coat
Late Edo period, 19th century
Paste resist-dyed plain-weave cotton, quilted
100.3 x 121.9 cm
John C. Weber Collection
PLATE 66

Sake Flask for Sumo
Edo period, 18th–19th century
Red, black and gold lacquer
26 x 32.8 x 6.9 cm
Brooklyn Museum of Art, Designated Purchase Fund

Woman's Robe
Meiji period, late19th-early 20th century
Spun silk
148.4 x 101.2 cm
Private Collection
PLATE 67

Woman's *Kosode* Robe
Late Edo period, 19th century
Stencil resist-dyed silk crepe
144.8 x 120.7 cm
Private Collection
PLATE 68

Woman's Summer *Kosode* Robe
Edo period, 19th century
Resist-dyed and painted plain-weave ramie
168.3 x 116.8 cm
John C. Weber Collection
PLATE 69

Woman's Three-quarter Length Jacket
Taisho period, early 20th century
Tie-dyed figured silk crepe
92.7 x 128.9 cm
John C. Weber Collection
PLATE 70

Geisha and Attendant by a River
Katsukawa Shuncho (active 1780-1795)
Edo period
Hanging scroll; ink, color and gold pigment on silk
96.2 x 35.2 cm
Signed: *Katsu Shuncho ga* and sealed *Sanko*
Private Collection

Inro
Style of Ogata Kōrin (1658–1716)
Edo period, 18th-19th century
Gold lacquer with lead and mother-of-pearl inlay;
soft-metal *ojime*, silk cord
5.7 x 5.1 cm
Philadelphia Museum of Art, Gift of Mrs. S. Emlen
Stokes (1987-25-2 a-e)
PLATE 71

Inro
Style of Ogata Kōrin (1658–1716)
Edo period, 18th–19th century
Black and gold lacquer with lead and mother-of-pearl
inlay
5.4 x 5.4 cm
Philadelphia Museum of Art, Gift of Mrs. S. Emlen
Stokes (1987-25-1 a,b,c)

Inro
Style of Ogata Kōrin (1658–1716)
Edo period, 18th–19th century
Gold lacquer with lead and mother-of-pearl inlay
6 x 5.3 cm
Philadelphia Museum of Art, Gift of Mrs. S. Emlen
Stokes (1987.25.3 a,b,c)

Inro
Shibata Zeshin (1807–1891)
Late Edo-early Meiji period
Gold and dark silver lacquer with polychrome
lacquer and scratched details, matching *ojime* and
netsuke, silk cord
9.6 x 7 cm
Signed: *Zeshin*
Kay and Tom Edson Collection
PLATE 72

Inro
Shibata Zeshin (1807–1891)
Late Edo-early Meiji period
Black lacquer with applied carved red lacquer
details, coral *ojime* and carved wood netsuke
9 x 6.2 cm
Signed: *Zeshin*
Kay and Tom Edson Collection

Smoking Set
Shibata Zeshin (1807–1891)
Late Edo-early Meiji period
Pipe: lacquered wood, iron, gold, silver
Pipe case: gold and black lacquer
Tobacco case: dyed cotton with leather backing, silk
cord, staghorn netsuke
Length of pipe case: 19.6 cm
Signed: *Zeshin*
The Florence and Herbert Irving Collection
PLATE 73

Pipe case
Hashimoto Ichizō (1817–1882)
Late Edo-early Meiji period
Lacquer on wood with gilt-metal fitting
Length: 18.2 cm
Signed: *Hashi'ichi*
Private Collection

Tobacco Pouch
Hashimoto Ichizō (1817–1882)
Late Edo period-early Meiji period
Lacquer over wood simulating bamboo
7.8 x 9 cm x 7.5 cm
Signed: *Hashimoto*
Private Collection

Pipe
Late Edo-early Meiji period, 19th century
Gold, iron
Length: 24.2 cm
Peabody-Essex Museum, Gift of C. G. Weld (E 9398)

Pipe
Edo period, late 18th–19th century
Shakudō, bamboo
Length: 43.7 cm
Peabody-Essex Museum, Gift of C. G. Weld, 1909 (E
12,610)

Tobacco Container
Edo period, 19th century
Negoro ware; red lacquer
7 x 6 cm
Peggy and Richard M. Danziger Collection
PLATE 75

Rice Measure, used as tobacco tray
Late Edo-Meiji period, late 19th–early 20th century
Zelkova wood
8.3 x 16.5 cm
Peggy and Richard M. Danziger Collection

Sake Cup Washer
Kitaoji Rosanjin (1883–1959)
Showa period
Porcelain painted with underglaze blue
Height: 11 cm; diameter: 8 cm
Signed: *ro*
Peggy and Richard M. Danziger Collection

Tobacco Tray
Edo period, 18th century
Kyoto ware, Ko Kiyomizu type; stoneware, cobalt-
blue underglaze and enamels
20 x 16.6 x 18.6 cm
Private Collection
PLATE 74

Set of Five *Mukōzuke* Dishes
Momoyama period, early 17th century
Mino ware, Oribe type; glazed stoneware, iron-oxide
design and copper-green glaze
2.7 x 9 x 5.1 cm
Peggy and Richard M. Danziger Collection
PLATE 80

Set of Five *Mukōzuke* Dishes
Edo period, 17th century
Arita ware; porcelain painted with underglaze
cobalt-blue
Each approximately 14.7 x 8.8 x 2.2 cm
Private Collection
PLATE 79

Ornamental Wooden Sword
Shibata Zeshin (1807–1891)
Late Edo-early Meiji period
Lacquered wood applied with gold and silver
lacquer, silver, copper, silk cord
44.3 x 3.8 x 1.2 cm
Signed: *Zeshin*
Private Collection
PLATE 77

Scabbard with Mounting
Shibata Zeshin (1807–1891)
Late Edo-early Meiji period (19th century)
Lacquered wood; fittings: black lacquer with gold
and brown lacquer decoration; *menuki*: gilt metal
41.9 x 4.7 x 6 cm
Signed: *Zeshin*
Private Collection
PLATE 76

Scabbard Maker's Shop Sign
Edo period, mid-19th century
Lacquered wood with iron, leather, shagreen and
shell inlay
66.8 x 27 cm
Peabody-Essex Museum, Gift, Friends of Peabody
Museum, 1916 (E.16,473)

Fire Warden's Shop Sign
Meiji period, early 20th century
Wood, pigment
29.2 x 76.3 cm
Private Collection
PLATE 81

Plaque for Ichikawa Danjurō, Kabuki Actor
Late Edo-early Meiji period, 19th century
Wood, pigment, metal hook
51 x 20 cm
Peabody-Essex Museum, Gift of E.S. Morse, 1898
(E 4168)
PLATE 82

Teahouse Sign
Edo period, 19th century
Wood, lacquer, shell and ceramic inlay
85 x 71 cm
Peabody-Essex Museum, Gift of C. L. Freer, 1908
(E 12,519)
PLATE 83

Comb Shop Sign
Meiji period, late 19th–early 20th century
Wood
100 x 130 cm
Steven and Jacqueline Strelitz Collection

Five-tiered Food Box
Shibata Zeshin (1807–1891)
Late Edo period
Gold lacquer on brown and green lacquer, silver,
mother-of-pearl inlay
41 x 22.8 x 24.4 cm
Kay and Tom Edson Collection
PLATE 78

Box
Koma Kōryūsai (active 18th century)
Mid-Edo period
Wood, polychrome lacquer, metal fittings
22.2 x 28.6 x 23.2 cm
Signed: *Koma Kōryūsai* and with cursive monogram
The Metropolitan Museum of Art, Edward C. Moore
Collection, Bequest of Edward C. Moore, 1891
(91.1.730)
PLATE 84

Further Reading

Aikens, C. Melvin, and Takayasu Higuchi. *Prehistory of Japan.* New York: Academic Press, 1982.

Becker, Johanna. *Karatsu Ware: A Tradition of Diversity.* New York and Tokyo: Kodansha International, 1986.

Brandon, Reiko Mochinaga. *Country Textiles of Japan: The Art of Tsutsugaki.* Exh. cat. Honolulu: Honolulu Academy of Arts; New York and Tokyo: Weatherhill, 1986.

Chadō Koten Zenshū (The complete classic tea ceremony). Compiled by Sōshitsu Sen. 12 vols. Kyoto: Tankōsha, 1961.

Cort, Louise Allison. *Shigaraki, Potters' Valley.* New York and Tokyo: Kodansha International, 1979.

Figgess, John. *The Heritage of Japanese Ceramics.* Translated and adapted from *Nihon Tōji no Dentō* by Fujio Koyama, with an introduction by John Alexander Pope. New York and Tokyo: Weatherhill; Kyoto: Tankōsha, 1973.

Ford, Barbara Brennan, and Oliver R. Impey. *Japanese Art from the Gerry Collection in The Metropolitan Museum of Art.* Exh. cat. New York: Metropolitan Museum of Art, 1989.

Fujisawa, Norio, and Emily J. Sano, eds. *Classical Kimono from the Kyoto National Museum: Four Centuries of Fashion.* Exh. cat. San Francisco: Asian Art Museum of San Francisco, 1997.

Furukawa, Shōsaku. *Kiseto and Setoguro.* Famous Ceramics of Japan, no. 10. New York and Tokyo: Kodansha International, 1983.

Furuto, Kazuie, et al., eds. *The Shogun Age Exhibition.* Exh. cat. Tokyo: Shogun Age Exhibition Executive Committee, 1983.

Gibney, Frank, Lea Sneider, Dana Levy. *Kanban: Shop Signs of Japan.* Exh. cat. New York: Japan Society; Weatherhill, 1983.

Gluckman, Dale Carolyn, and Sharon Sadako Takeda. *When Art Became Fashion: Kosode in Edo-Period Japan.* Exh. cat. Los Angeles: Los Angeles County Museum of Art; New York: Weatherhill, 1992.

Guth, Christine. *The Art of Edo Japan: The Artist and the City, 1615–1868.* Perspectives. New York: Harry N. Abrams, Inc., 1996.

Gōke Tadaomi, ed. Shibata Zeshin meihinshū: Bakumatsu kaikaki no shikkō kaiga *(Masterpieces by Shibata Zeshin: Painting and Lacquerware from the Late Edo Period).* 2 vols, Tokyo: Gakken, 1981.

Hauge, Victor, and Takako Hauge. *Folk Traditions in Japanese Art.* Exh. cat. DC: IEF New York and Tokyo: Kodansha International, 1978.

Hayashiya, Seizō. *Chanoyu: Japanese Tea Ceremony.* Translated by Emily J. Sano. Exh. cat. New York: Japan Society, 1979.

_____, ed. *Nihon no tōji* (Japanese Ceramics). 14 vols. Tokyo: Chūkō kōron-sha, 1971-90.

The Heibosha Survey of Japanese Art, 31 vols. Tokyo and New York: Weatherhill and Heibonsha, 1971-80.

Hickman, Money L., et al. *Japan's Golden Age: Momoyama,* Exh. cat. Dallas: Dallas Museum of Art and New Haven: Yale University Press, 1996.

Hume, Nancy G., ed. *Japanese Aesthetics and Culture: A Reader.* Albany, NY: State University of New York Press, 1995.

Imanaga, Seiji, and Ken Kirihata, eds. *Kosode. Nihon no Senshoku* (Japanese textiles), vols. 5 and 6. Edited by Tomoyuki Yamanobe. Tokyo: Chūō Kō ron-sha 1983 .

Imamura, Keiji. *Prehistoric Japan: New Perspectives on Insular East Asia.* London: University College of London Press, 1996.

Ishimura, Hayao, and Nobuhiko Maruyama. *Robes of Elegance: Japanese Kimonos of the 16th-20th Centuries.* Translated by Haruko Ward. Exh. cat. Raleigh: North Carolina Museum of Art, 1988.

Itōh, Teiji, Ikkō Tanaka, and Tsune Sesoko, eds. *Wabi, Sabi, Suki: The Essence of Japanese Culture.* Hiroshima, Japan: Mazda Motor Co., 1993.

Jackson, Anna. *Japanese Country Textiles.* Exh. cat. Victoria and Albert Museum Far Eastern Series. London: Victoria and Albert Museum Publications, New York and Tokyo: Weatherhill, 1997.

Kidder, Edward J. *The Art of Japan.* New York: Park Lane, 1985.

_____. *Early Japanese Art: The Great Tombs and Treasures.* London: Thames and Hudson, 1964.

The Kojiki: Records of Ancient Matters. Translated by Basil Hall Chamberlain. Rutland, VT: Charles E. Tuttle, 1981.

Kuki, Shūzō. *Reflections on Japanese Taste: The Structure of Iki.* Translated by John Clark. Sydney, Australia: Power Publications, 1997.

Kuroda, Ryōji. *Shino.* Famous Ceramics of Japan, no. 12. New York and Tokyo: Kodansha International, 1984.

Leidy, Denise Patry. *Treasures of Asian Art: The Asia Society's Mr. and Mrs. John D. Rockefeller 3rd Collection.* New York: Asia Society Galleries, 1994.

Lee, Sherman E. *Tea Taste in Japanese Art.* Exh. cat. New York: Asia House, 1963.

Maruyama, Nobuhiko. "Edo Fuasshon Jijō: Ryukō to Egakareta Yosooi" (Edo fashion: Popular trends as seen in dress). In *Edo no Fuasshon: Nikuhitsu Ukiyo-e ni Miru Onnatachi no Yosooi* (Fashion of Edo: Women's dress in ukiyo-e paintings). Exh. cat. Tokyo: Azabu Musuem of Arts and Crafts, 1989.

Mingei: Masterpieces of Japanese Folkcraft. Exh. cat. New York and Tokyo: Kodansha International, 1991.

Mingei: Two Centuries of Japanese Folk Art. Edited by the International Programs Department, Japan Folk Crafts Museum. Exh. cat. Tokyo: Japan Folk Crafts Museum, 1995. Rev. ed. 1998.

Minnich, Helen Benton in collaboration with Shōjiro Nomura. *Japanese Costume and the Makers of Its Elegant Tradition.* Rutland, VT: Charles E. Tuttle Co., 1963.

Mizoguchi, Saburō. *Design Motifs*. Translated and adapted by Louise Allison Cort. Arts of Japan, vol. 1. New York: Weatherhill; Tokyo: Shibundo, 1973.

Moes, Robert, and Amanda Stinchecum. *Japanese Folk Art: A Triumph of Simplicity from the Montgomery Collection*. New York: Japan Society, 1992.

Moes, Robert. *Mingei: Japanese Folk Art*. Exh. cat. Alexandria, VA: Art Services International, 1995.

Murase, Miyeko. *Bridge of Dreams: The Mary Griggs Burke Collection of Japanese Art*. New York: Metropolitan Museum of Art, 2000.

_____. *Jewel Rivers: Japanese Art from the Burke Collection*. Exh. Cat. Richmond: Virginia Museum of Fine Arts, 1993.

Murayama, Takeshi. *Oribe*. Famous Ceramics of Japan, no. 8. New York and Tokyo: Kodansha International, 1982.

Nagasaki, Iwao, ed. "Chōnin no Fukushoku" (Merchant's clothing), no. 341. *Nihon no bijutsu* (Arts of Japan), no. 10. Tokyo: Shibundo, 1994.

Nagasaki, Iwao. *Kosode*. Kyoto Shoin's Art Library of Japanese Textiles, vol. 4. Kyoto: Kyoto Shoin, 1993.

Newland, Joseph N., ed. *Japanese Bamboo Baskets: Masterworks of Form and Texture from The Collection of Lloyd Cotsen*. Los Angeles: Cotsen Occasional Press, 1999.

Nishimura, Hyōbu, Jean Mailey, and Joseph S. Hayes, Jr. *Tagasode: Whose Sleeves: Kimono from the Kanebō Collection*. Exh. cat. New York: Japan Society, 1976.

Ogawa, Morihiro. *Japanese Swords and Sword Furniture in the Museum of Fine Arts, Boston (Bosuton Bijutsukan zō Nihontō Tōsō Tōsō gushū.)* Tokyo: Ōtsuka Kōgeisha, 1984.

Ōhara, Tetsuo, ed. *Mōsu no Mita Nihon: Seiramu Pībodī Hakubutsukan zō Mōsu Korekushon: Nihon Mingu hen* (Japan, through the eyes of E. S. Morse: Peabody Museum of Salem Morse Collection, Japanese folk crafts). Exh. cat. Translated by Etsuko Ōhashi. Tokyo: Shōgakkan, 1988.

Okakura, Kakuzō. *The Book of Tea*. New York and Tokyo: Kodansha International, 1989.

Pearson, Richard J. *Ancient Japan*. Exh. cat. New York: George Braziller; Washington, D.C.: Arthur M. Sackler Gallery, 1992.

_____ et al. *The Rise of a Great Tradition: Japanese Archaeological Ceramics from the Jōmon through Heian Periods*. Exh. cat. New York: Japan Society; Tokyo: Agency for Cultural Affairs, Government of Japan, 1990.

Pekarik, Andrew. *Japanese Lacquer, 1600-1900: Selections from the Charles A. Greenfield Collection*. Exh. cat. New York: Metropolitan Museum of Art, 1980.

Rathbun, William Jay. *Beyond the Tanabata Bridge: Traditional Japanese Textiles*. Exh. cat. Seattle, WA: Seattle Art Museum, 1993.

_____. *Yō no Bi: The Beauty of Japanese Folk Art*. Exh. cat. Seattle, WA: Seattle Art Museum; University of Washington Press, 1983.

Seigle, Cecilia Segawa. *Yoshiwara: The Glittering World of the Japanese Courtesan*. Honolulu: University of Hawaii Press, 1993.

Shimizu, Yoshiaki, ed. *Japan: The Shaping of Daimyō Culture, 1185-1868*. Exh. cat. Washington, D.C.: National Gallery of Art, 1988.

Singer, Robert T., et al. *Edo Art in Japan 1615-1868*. Exh. cat. Washington, D.C.: National Gallery of Art, 1998.

Stinchecum, Amanda Mayer. *Kosode: 16th–19th Century Textiles from the Nomura Collection*. Exh. cat. New York: Japan Society, 1984.

Takashina, Shuji, Masakazu Yamazaki, Shigenobu Kimura, and Toyomune Minamoto, et al. *From the Suntory Museum of Art: Autumn Grasses and Water Motifs in Japanese Art*. Exh. cat. Translated by Hiroaki Sato. New York: Japan Society; Tokyo: The Suntory Museum of Art, 1983.

Ueda, Makoto. *Literary and Art Theories in Japan*. Cleveland, Ohio: Press of Western Reserve University, 1967. Reprint. Ann Arbor: Center for Japanese Studies, University of Michigan, 1991.

Varley, Paul H. *Japanese Culture*. 3rd ed. Honolulu:uuUniversity of Hawaii Press, 1984.

_____ and Kumakura Isao, eds. *Tea in Japan: Essays in the History of Chanoyu*. Honolulu: University of Hawaii Press, 1984.

Watson, William, ed. *The Great Japan Exhibition: Art of the Edo Period, 1600-1868*. Exh. cat. London: Royal Academy of Arts, 1981.

Watt, James C.Y., and Barbara Brennan Ford. *East Asian Lacquer: The Florence and Herbert Irving Collection*. Exh. cat. New York: Metropolitan Museum of Art, 1991.

Wilson, Richard L. *The Art of Ogata Kenzan: Persona and Production in Japanese Ceramics*. New York: Weatherhill, 1991.

Yanagi, Sōetsu. *The Unknown Craftsman: A Japanese Insight into Beauty*. Adapted by Bernard Leach. Foreword by Shōji Hamada. Palo Alto, Cal. and Tokyo: Kodansha International, 1972.

Yonemura, Ann. *Japanese Lacquer*. Washington, D.C.: Freer Gallery of Art, Smithsonian Institution, 1979.

Prepared by Megumi Saito Lincoln